CORS TRAVEL GUIDE 2023 2024

A CAPTIVATNG TRAVEL GUIDE TO THE ENCHANTING JEWEL OF FRANCE

ISLAND KING J

copyright© ISLAND KING J
2023
All rights reserved.

Welcome to Corsica _____8

*Five reasons why you should visit Corsica*_____10

Introduction _____11

*CHAPTER ONE*_____13

Overview of Corsica_____13

Becoming acquainted with the Island of Corsica_____16

Geography _____16
Climate _____17
Demographics _____18
Population _____18
Language _____18
Age Distribution _____19
Economy_____19
Corsican Culture and Identity _____20
Geographical features _____21
Corsican History and Culture _____24
Artisans and traditional crafts _____25
Culinary traditions _____25
Sense of Community _____26
Corsican Language _____27
Historical Background _____28

CHAPTER TWO _____31

Planning your trip _____31

Best Time to Visit _____31
Visa and Travel Requirements _____33
Accommodation Options _____35
Currency and Banking _____45
Language and Communication _____47
How to Get to Corsica _____48

CHAPTER THREE _____53

Exploring the Regions of Corsica_____53

Sanguinaires Islands _____56
Gulf Valinco _____57
Bastia City _____59
Cap Corse Peninsula_____60

2

Nebbio Region _____61
Balagne and Calvi _____62
Piana Calanques _____63
Porto-Vecchio and the South Coast _____64
Bonifacio and Lavezzi Islands _____65
Alta Rocca Area _____66
Corte and the Central Mountains _____67
Restonica Valley _____68
Castagniccia Region _____68

Must-Visit Destinations_____70
Bonifacio_____70
King of Aragon's Staircase _____71
Lavezzi Islands _____72
Porto_____73
Aiguilles de Bavella_____79
L'Île-Rousse_____81
Pietra Lighthouse _____82

Outdoor Activities _____83
Routes for Hiking and Trekking _____83
Beaches and Water Sports_____86
Snorkeling and Diving Spot _____87
Water Sports and boat rentals_____88
Rock Climbing and Canyoning _____89
Boating and Sailing_____92
Day Trips and Coastal Cruises _____93
Wildlife Watching_____94

*CHAPTER FOUR*_____97

Corsican Dining and Cuisine _____97
Corsican charcuterie_____97
Fiadone and Other Desserts_____98

Popular Local Restaurants _____99
Restaurant Recommendations in Ajaccio _____99
Restaurant Recommendations in Bastia _____100
Restaurant Recommendations in Calvi _____100

Wine and Local Drinks_____101
Corsican Wine Regions and Varietals_____101
Tasting Tours and Vineyard Visits _____102

Culinary Events and Festivals _____ **104**
Chestnut Fairs _____ 104
Seafood and Fishermen Festivals _____ 105
Wine and Gastronomy Events _____ 106

Cultural Experiences _____ **107**
Music and Festivals in Corsica _____ 107

Traditional Arts and Crafts _____ **109**
Corsican Knife Making _____ 109
Ceramics and Pottery _____ 110
Art Galleries and Craft Work _____ 111

Museums and historical sites _____ **112**
Ajaccio's Napoleon Bonaparte Sites _____ 112
The Fesch Museum _____ 113
Corsican Resistance Museum _____ 113

Shopping and Local Markets _____ **114**
Ajaccio Market _____ 115
Bastia Market _____ 115
Shopping Tips for Local Products _____ 116

Packing Essentials _____ **117**
Clothing and Footwear _____ 117
Outdoor Gear and Equipment _____ 119
Toiletries and Personal Items _____ 120
Miscellaneous _____ 120
Other electronic gadgets _____ 121

Customs and Etiquette _____ **122**
Social Customs and Greetings _____ 122
Tipping and Service Charges _____ 123
Useful Phrases and Vocabulary _____ 124

CHAPTER FIVE _____ **125**

Corsica with Kids _____ **125**
Family-Friendly Activities _____ 125
Child-Friendly Beaches _____ 126
Attractions and Theme Parks _____ 127
Kid-Friendly Accommodation _____ 127

Corsica's Nightlife _____ **128**

Nightclubs and Bars _____128
Live Music and Entertainment _____129
Cultural Evening Events _____130

Where to Buy Fashion and Design wears_____131
Fashion Boutiques in Corsica _____131
Home Design and Decor Stores _____132

Corsica's Hidden Gems _____133
Remote and Secluded Beaches _____133
Hidden Coves and Swimming Holes_____134
Charming Hilltop Villages _____135
Remote Mountain Retreats _____137

Travel Itineraries _____142
A detailed 7 days itinerary _____142
A detailed 3 three days itinerary _____144
Reliable book source for your Corsica travel _____146
Emergency contact numbers _____147
30 dos and don'ts for your Corsica travel _____148

10 important money saving tips_____151
Best time to travel to Corsica for the best prices _____152

20 Important Safety Tips_____153

CHAPTER SIX _____156

Conclusion _____156

5

Welcome to Corsica

I have always been captivated by the allure of travel, and when the opportunity arose to explore the enchanting island of Corsica, I couldn't resist. With excitement bubbling inside me, I embarked on a journey that would forever etch itself in my heart.

As the plane touched down on Corsican soil, I felt a surge of anticipation. Stepping off the aircraft, I was immediately enveloped by the island's natural beauty. The scent of wildflowers filled the air, and a gentle breeze carried with it whispers of adventure.

Throughout my time in Corsica, I encountered a warmth and friendliness that surpassed all expectations. From the bustling streets of Bastia to the tranquil villages tucked away in the mountains, the locals embraced me as if I were an old friend. Their genuine smiles and heartfelt conversations created an instant connection, making me feel at home in this faraway place.

Corsica's landscape proved to be a masterpiece of nature's design. I hiked along rugged trails that wound through majestic mountains, the scent of pine, and the song of birds accompanying my every step. The vistas that greeted me at every turn were nothing short of breathtaking—rolling hills covered in vibrant greenery, dramatic cliffs cascading into crystal-clear waters, and hidden coves where time seemed to stand still.

One particular moment stands out in my memory: a visit to the picturesque village of Corte. As I strolled through its narrow streets, I marveled at the centuries-old buildings adorned with colorful shutters and blooming flowers. The locals' passion for their heritage was evident in every corner, from the lively markets showcasing local crafts and delicacies to the music that echoed through the air during traditional festivals.

Corsica's allure extended to its culinary delights. I savored the taste of fresh seafood, indulged in hearty mountain cuisine, and discovered the island's famed charcuterie. Each bite was a journey in itself—a symphony of flavors that reflected the island's rich cultural tapestry.

But what truly made my time in Corsica unforgettable were the people I encountered along the way. They shared their stories, their traditions, and their heartfelt pride in their island. Whether it was an elderly shepherd guiding me through the rugged terrain or a jovial local at a bustling café, their genuine hospitality left an indelible mark on my soul.

As my departure date approached, a mix of emotions washed over me. Gratitude for the memories and connections forged, a longing to stay just a little longer, and a profound sense of appreciation for the world's vast wonders. Corsica had not only gifted me with awe-inspiring landscapes but had taught me the power of human connection and the joy of embracing new experiences.

As I boarded the plane to return home, I knew that Corsica had become a part of me. Its spirit would forever reside within, guiding me on future adventures and reminding me of the warmth and beauty that lies in venturing beyond one's comfort zone.

Corsica, a place that had once seemed distant and unknown, had become a cherished chapter in the story of my life—a story filled with breathtaking landscapes, friendly faces, and the transformative power of travel.

10

Five reasons why you should visit Corsica

1. Breathtaking Natural Beauty: Corsica is renowned for its stunning natural landscapes, from pristine beaches with crystal-clear waters to dramatic mountain capes. The island offers diverse outdoor activities, including hiking along picturesque trails, exploring hidden coves, and enjoying water sports such as snorkeling and kayaking. Whether you're a nature enthusiast or simply seeking tranquility, Corsica's awe-inspiring beauty will leave you in awe.

2. Rich Cultural Heritage: Corsica is steeped in fascinating history and boasts a unique blend of French and Italian influences. Explore charming villages with their ancient stone houses, visit historical sites such as the citadel in Bonifacio, or wander through the vibrant cities of Ajaccio and Bastia. Immerse yourself in Corsican culture by attending lively festivals, tasting traditional cuisine, and learning about the island's rich folklore.

3. Exquisite Cuisine and Wine: Corsican gastronomy is a true delight for food enthusiasts. Indulge in a variety of mouthwatering dishes, from the island's renowned charcuterie featuring cured meats and artisanal cheeses to fresh seafood caught in the surrounding Mediterranean waters. Don't forget to pair your meal with a glass of local wine, as Corsica's vineyards produce exceptional reds, whites, and rosés.

4. Warm Hospitality: The people of Corsica are known for their warm and friendly nature. You'll be greeted with genuine hospitality and a willingness to share their island's treasures. Engage in conversations with locals, who will gladly provide recommendations for hidden gems and share their personal stories. The warmth and kindness of the Corsican people will make your trip all the more memorable.

5. Diverse Experiences: Corsica offers a range of activities to suit every traveler's interests. The island caters to diverse preferences, whether you're seeking relaxation on pristine beaches, outdoor adventures in the mountains, cultural exploration in charming villages, or gastronomic delights. From hiking and water sports to wine tasting and historical tours, Corsica provides a well-rounded experience that can be tailored to your preferences.

With its natural beauty, cultural heritage, delicious cuisine, warm hospitality, and diverse experiences, Corsica is a destination that will captivate your senses and create cherished memories. It's time to start planning your next vacation to this enchanting Mediterranean island.

Introduction

Welcome to Corsica travel guide: A Captivating Travel Guide to the Enchanting Jewel of France Prepare to embark on a remarkable journey through the hidden treasures of Corsica, a mesmerizing island nestled in the Mediterranean Sea.

As you turn the pages of this guide, allow us to transport you to a world where rugged mountains meet pristine beaches, where ancient history and vibrant culture coexist harmoniously. Corsica, often referred to as the "Enchanting Jewel of France," awaits your exploration.

Our guide will lead you through the diverse landscapes and experiences that Corsica has to offer. From the bustling streets of Ajaccio to the serene villages nestled in the mountains, you will discover the soul of this captivating island. Unveil its secrets as you wander through ancient citadels perched atop dramatic cliffs, visit charming vineyards producing exceptional wines, and indulge in the tantalizing flavors of Corsican cuisine.

Corsica's natural beauty will leave you breathless. Explore secluded coves with crystal-clear waters, hike along picturesque trails that wind through lush forests, and marvel at the panoramic views from towering peaks. Allow the tranquility of the island to envelop you, as you immerse yourself in its pristine nature.

But it's not just the landscapes that make Corsica truly captivating; it's the warmth and hospitality of its people. Engage in conversations with locals, who will proudly share their stories, traditions, and love for their island. Experience Corsican culture firsthand through lively festivals, traditional crafts, and the echoes of history that resonate throughout the island.

Corsica travel guide: A Captivating Travel Guide to the Enchanting Jewel of France is your trusted companion on this remarkable journey. With detailed insider tips and captivating storytelling, we aim to enhance your experience and help you create memories that will last a lifetime.

So, embark on this captivating adventure and let Corsica work its magic on you. Unveil the enchanting jewel of France, a destination that promises to captivate your heart, ignite your senses, and leave you longing for more. Let the pages of this guide be your gateway to the extraordinary world of Corsica.

CHAPTER ONE
Overview of Corsica

Corsica, the dazzling island in the Mediterranean Sea, is a treasure trove of natural wonders, rich history, and vibrant culture. Located southeast of mainland France and west of Italy, this stunning island captivates visitors with its diverse landscapes, pristine beaches, charming villages, and rugged mountains.

Geographically, Corsica showcases a unique blend of coastal beauty and mountainous terrain. The island boasts a coastline stretching over 1,000 kilometers, offering a plethora of picturesque beaches. From the renowned Palombaggia and Rondinara beaches with their turquoise waters and soft sand to the secluded and unspoiled Plage de Saleccia and Plage de Santa Giulia, Corsica's shores cater to every beach lover's desires. The island also houses enchanting calanques—narrow fjord-like inlets—such as the Calanques de Piana, adorned with striking red granite cliffs that rise dramatically from the azure waters.

Inland, Corsica's landscape is dominated by the Corsican Mountains, part of the larger Alpine chain. The mountains are characterized by rugged peaks, deep valleys, and dense forests that make them a haven for outdoor enthusiasts. The famous GR20 trail, considered one of Europe's most challenging long-distance hikes, traverses the island from north to south, taking intrepid hikers through breathtaking scenery, including glacial lakes, roaring rivers, and panoramic vistas. The tranquil Restonica Valley and the rugged Bavella

Massif are just a few of the many natural gems awaiting exploration in the island's mountainous interior.

Corsica's historical and cultural heritage is equally captivating. The island has a complex past, having been influenced by various civilizations throughout history. From prehistoric sites to Roman ruins, Genoese fortresses to medieval citadels, Corsica's historical landmarks are a testament to its vibrant past. Bonifacio, perched atop towering cliffs, is a sight to behold with its well-preserved medieval old town and citadel. Ajaccio, the birthplace of Napoleon Bonaparte, offers visitors a glimpse into the island's history and the chance to explore the Maison Bonaparte, the ancestral home of the famous French emperor.

Corsica's charming villages, scattered throughout the island, provide a glimpse into the island's traditional way of life. Wander through the cobblestone streets of Corte, the historic capital, and explore its ancient university and imposing citadel. Visit the hilltop village of Sartène, known as the "most Corsican of Corsican towns," with its stone houses and vibrant local culture. The quaint village of Calvi boasts a beautiful beach, a picturesque marina, and a charming old town that invites leisurely strolls and delightful discoveries.

Corsican cuisine is a delicious fusion of French and Italian flavors, showcasing the island's agricultural abundance and proximity to the sea. Indulge in the island's renowned charcuterie, featuring flavorful cured meats like lonzu and coppa, complemented by artisanal cheeses such as brocciu and casgiu merzu. Sample local specialties like wild boar stew, chestnut-based delicacies, and the unique fiadone, a

16

traditional Corsican cheesecake. Wash it all down with a glass of Corsican wine, produced from local grape varieties in vineyards that dot the island's landscape.

Corsica's warm and welcoming atmosphere adds a special touch to any visit. The Corsican people, known for their pride in their island, greet visitors with genuine hospitality and a sense of community. Engage in conversations with locals, and you'll discover their passion for Corsica's traditions, music, and language. The island's festivals, such as the lively Fête de la Saint-Jean and the traditional polyphonic singing gatherings, provide opportunities to immerse yourself in Corsican culture and create unforgettable memories.

Whether you seek outdoor adventures, cultural immersion, or simply a peaceful retreat in a breathtaking setting, Corsica has it all. With its stunning landscapes, rich history, delectable cuisine, and warm-hearted locals, this enchanting island is sure to leave a lasting impression on every traveler fortunate enough to explore its treasures.

Becoming acquainted with the Island of Corsica

Geography

Corsica, sometimes known as the "Island of Beauty," is a Mediterranean treasure in the western Mediterranean Sea. It is located southeast of the French mainland, west of Italy, and north of Sardinia. With an area of around 8,700 square kilometers, the island is the fourth-largest in the Mediterranean.

Corsica's topography is distinguished by its various landscapes, which include breathtaking coasts, steep mountains, and beautiful valleys. The coastline of the island runs for nearly 1,000 kilometers and is dotted with sandy beaches, secret coves, and stunning cliffs. The Corsican Mountains, part of the Alpine range, dominate the interior, with Monte Cinto being the highest peak at 2,706 meters above sea level. These mountains are home to steep gorges, gushing waterfalls, and lush woods, making them ideal for trekking, climbing, and canyoning.

Corsica has various rivers and lakes in addition to its stunning coastline and rugged landscape. The crystal-clear waters of the Restonica River slice through the granite terrain, producing picturesque swimming holes and natural pools. Corsica's lakes, such as Lac de Melu and Lac de Capitello, are tucked away among the mountains, providing peaceful settings for leisure and exploration.

Climate

Corsica has a Mediterranean, characterized by mild, wet winters and warm, dry summers. However, owing to the island's varied geography, microclimates vary dramatically throughout various places.

Summers in coastal locations, especially on the east coast, are often hot and dry, with temperatures frequently exceeding 30°C (86°F) or more. The sea wind offers a welcome relief from the heat, making it a great time for beach activities and water sports Winters along the coast are mild, with temperatures seldom falling below 10°C (50°F), allowing for comfortable outdoor exploration.

The environment grows colder and more unpredictable as you go further into the mountainous core. Temperatures are cooler at higher elevations, particularly during the winter months, when snowfall is widespread. Spring and fall in the mountains have pleasant weather, making them ideal seasons for trekking and enjoying the beautiful vistas.

Corsica gets a lot of rain, especially during the colder months. Mountains, in particular, attract clouds and precipitation, resulting in a greener environment and a greater variety of water sources. Corsica's natural beauty is at its best in the spring, with its blossoming wildflowers and running streams.

Corsica's climate overall provides a great blend of warm summers and moderate winters, making it a year-round destination for outdoor activities, cultural discovery, and leisure.

Corsica's diversified terrain and favorable climate add to its popularity as a sought-after destination for nature lovers, adventure seekers, and those seeking a calm getaway among stunning scenery. Corsica's terrain and climate offer the ideal background for an amazing adventure, whether you're exploring the coasts, climbing the summits, or immersing yourself in the island's cultural legacy.

Demographics

Corsica, being a French region, forms part of the country's greater demographic profile. However, several distinguishing factors contribute to the island's distinct demography.

Population

Corsica's population is estimated to be at 330,000 people. The density of people varies over the island, with denser populations found near the coast and in bigger towns and cities.

Language

Corsicans are mostly of Italian and French heritage, reflecting the island's historical links to both nations. Corsicans have a strong sense of identity and take pride in their own culture and customs. A segment of the population, especially in rural regions, speaks the Corsican language, a variation of Italian. However, French is the official language of the island and is widely spoken and understood.

The population of Corsica is divided equally between urban and rural regions. The bigger cities, like as Ajaccio (the capital), Bastia, and Calvi, draw a sizable population and provide urban conveniences, cultural attractions, and economic prospects. Small towns and hamlets dot the countryside, especially in the hilly interior, where a more traditional way of life prevails.

Age Distribution

Corsica's age distribution, like that of many affluent countries, displays an aging population. However, the island boasts a sizable population of young people, notably in metropolitan areas and university cities. This age mix adds to a dynamic and diversified community.

Economy

The economy of Corsica is primarily driven by industries like as tourism, agriculture, and services. The natural beauty and cultural richness of the island attract people from all over the globe, adding to the importance of the tourism sector. Agriculture is important, with noteworthy agricultural exports including wine, cheese, olive oil, and chestnuts. The transportation, hotel, and retail industries all contribute to the local economy.

Corsica is subject to both internal and external migration trends. Internal migration occurs when individuals relocate across areas of France in search of economic opportunities or a change in lifestyle. Individuals from other nations who choose to reside on the island are enticed by its particular charm and quality of life.

Overall, the demographics of Corsica indicate a mix of cultural influences, a strong sense of local identity, and a diversified population dispersed between urban and rural regions. The demographics of the island, as well as its breathtaking terrain, active culture, and pleasant temperature, add to its special charm and make it a popular destination for both tourists and inhabitants.

Corsican Culture and Identity

Corsican identity and culture are strongly ingrained in the island's history, terrain, and people's endurance. Corsicans are proud of their particular past, which is influenced by a mix of Italian and French influences, as well as their own peculiar customs.

A strong feeling of regional pride and a desire to conserve and develop Corsican culture are often associated with Corsican identity. The Corsicans are known for their independence and strong connection to their country. The harsh and untamed landscapes of the island, from its mountain peaks to its beautiful beaches, have ingrained in Corsicans a love and respect for nature.

The Corsican language is an important part of Corsican culture. Corsican, an Italian dialect, is spoken by a part of the population and is designated as a regional language. It is very important in retaining the island's particular character and is often employed in cultural events, music, and literature.

Another treasured feature of the island's cultural legacy is Corsican music, notably polyphonic singing. Polyphonic chants, chanted by numerous voices without musical accompaniment, feature evocative melodies and harmonies that have been handed down through centuries. These ancient melodies encapsulate the spirit of Corsica, expressing pride, desire, and a strong connection with the country.

Corsican cuisine is a delectable blend of French and Italian tastes that highlights the island's agricultural abundance and culinary heritage. Local ingredients such as chestnuts, olives, honey, and herbs are combined to make delectable recipes. Corsican charcuterie, which includes cured meats such as lonzu and coppa, as well as artisanal cheeses such as brocciu and casgiu merzu, is highly respected for its quality and flavor. Corsicans take great pleasure in sharing their culinary delicacies, which are often complemented by a glass of Corsican wine made from indigenous grape varietals.

Corsica's cultural calendar is filled with vibrant festivals and events that honor the island's customs and heritage. One such celebration is the Fête de la Saint-Jean, when bonfires are lighted over the island to celebrate the summer solstice. Music festivals, traditional processions, and local markets highlight Corsica's unique cultural tapestry.

Corsicans are likewise very attached to historical monuments and locations. Corsica's rich history is on show, from prehistoric megalithic buildings to Roman remains and Genoese fortifications to picturesque hilltop towns and citadels. Napoleon Bonaparte, the island's most famous son, adds another dimension to Corsican pride since the French emperor was born at Ajaccio.

Corsican identity is inextricably linked to a love of their land, a connection to nature, a feeling of community, and a desire to maintain their own culture. Corsican identity and culture are enthralling and valued because of their unique combination of history, geography, customs, and the tenacious spirit of their people.

Geographical features

Corsica, sometimes known as the "Island of Beauty," has a varied variety of geographical elements that add to its enchantment. Corsica has a variety of natural beauty to discover and enjoy, from towering mountains and rocky peaks to magnificent coastline panoramas and tranquil rivers and lakes.

Mountains

The Corsican Mountains, which are part of the broader Alpine group, dominate the scenery of the island. These towering peaks provide a stunning background and exceptional chances for outdoor pursuits. The tallest peak, Monte Cinto, rises 2,706 meters above sea level, highlighting the island's great heights. Paglia Orba, Capu Tafunatu, and Monte Renoso are further prominent summits.

Corsica's hilly interior is distinguished by deep valleys, steep gorges, and thick woods. Hikers, climbers, and nature lovers will love the challenging terrain. The famed GR20 hiking path, regarded as one of Europe's most difficult, crosses the island, transporting travelers through stunning landscapes and providing panoramic views of the surrounding mountains.

Coastal Landscapes
The coastline of Corsica runs for almost 1,000 kilometers adorned with an array of captivating landscapes. The island's coastline splendor is breathtaking, from sandy beaches and secret coves to towering cliffs and beautiful bays.

Palombaggia, Rondinara, and Santa Giulia are some of the most beautiful sandy beaches on the east coast. These beaches have crystal-clear turquoise seas and pure white sand, making them ideal for sunbathing, swimming, and water sports.

The western shore has more rough and wild terrain, with stunning cliffs and rocky outcrops. The UNESCO World Heritage site of the Calanques de Piana, with its characteristic red granite cliffs carved by wind and water, is a must-see for its spectacular beauty.

The coastline of Corsica is also peppered with lovely fishing villages and coastal towns. Bonifacio, built on towering limestone cliffs, has a lovely port and a well-preserved medieval old town, as well as stunning views of the Mediterranean Sea. Calvi blends natural beauty and historical appeal with its sandy beach, marina, and fortress.

Lakes and rivers

The rivers and lakes of Corsica give another layer of natural beauty to the island's environment. The Restonica River, which flows through the island's core, carves a route through granite cliffs, producing peaceful pools and soothing cascades. The river's crystal-clear waters are ideal for swimming, river walking, and picnics in tranquil settings.

The lakes of Corsica, situated among the mountains, provide tranquil settings for rest and exploration. Lac de Melo and Lac de Capitello, both situated in the Restonica Valley, are popular hiking and ecological sites. These alpine lakes, surrounded by towering peaks and rich foliage, provide a peaceful respite from the crowded coastal districts.

Corsica's rivers and lakes also play an important part in maintaining the island's diverse flora and wildlife. They provide habitat for a variety of animals, and the surrounding landscapes are ideal for birding and wildlife viewing.

Corsica's physical characteristics, such as its towering mountains, attractive coastline, and tranquil canals, combine to provide a perfect combination of natural treasures. Corsica's various landscapes will capture your senses and leave an unmistakable impression on your voyage, whether you want adventure in the mountains, leisure on sandy beaches, or a calm retreat by a river or lake.

Corsican History and Culture

Corsican traditions and customs are strongly established in the rich history and cultural legacy of the island. These age-old rituals have been handed down through generations, maintaining the Corsican people's distinct character. Corsica's customs, from colorful festivals and traditional rites to culinary traditions and local handicrafts, provide a look into the island's complex cultural tapestry.

Celebrations & Festivals

Corsicans commemorate their cultural history throughout the year with a variety of festivals and festivities. These festivities include traditional music, dance, costumes, and rituals, allowing both residents and tourists to immerse themselves in Corsican culture.

The Festival of Corsican Polyphony, held yearly in Calvi, is one of the most prominent events. This concert features famous Corsican choirs and singers performing traditional polyphonic chants, a unique kind of vocal music distinguished by many voices singing in harmony without instrumental accompaniment.

Other celebrations include the Fête de la Saint-Jean, which is celebrated with bonfires and processions on the summer solstice, and the Fête de la Saint-Érasme near Bonifacio, which honors the patron saint of fishermen with a colorful marine procession.

Artisans and traditional crafts

Corsica is home to talented craftsmen who preserve ancient crafts. From woodcarving and ceramics to weaving and knife-making, these craftsmen demonstrate their skills while helping to preserve Corsican craftsmanship.

Corsican knives, known as "curnicciulu" or "curniciellu," These intricately designed knives are not only practical tools but also bear symbolic significance in Corsican culture. The blades often feature engraved motifs representing local flora, fauna, or historical emblems.

Basket weaving is another ancient skill done in Corsica for ages. Natural materials such as chestnut branches, reeds, and straw are used by skilled craftsmen to make elegant and effective baskets that serve both ornamental and utilitarian functions.

Culinary traditions

Corsican cuisine is renowned for its delicious flavors and the use of fresh, locally sourced ingredients. Traditional Corsican dishes highlight the island's agricultural abundance and reflect a blend of Italian and French influences.

Charcuterie, which includes cured meats such as lonzu (pork tenderloin) and coppa (pork shoulder), is a popular dish in Corsica. These meats are seasoned with fragrant herbs and spices before being air-dried to provide rich tastes and soft textures.

Brocciu, a fresh sheep or goat milk cheese, is a popular Corsican ingredient. It's used in everything from savory meals like the famed "fiadone" (a cheese and lemon pie) to sweet treats like "canistrelli" (Corsican biscuits).

Chestnuts, a primary crop in Corsica, are used in soups, stews, and sweets. The island's chestnut flour, known as "farine de châtaigne," is extremely treasured and serves as the foundation for traditional Corsican bread and pastries.

Sense of Community

Corsicans have a strong feeling of community, as seen by their traditions and way of life. Family relationships are strongly treasured, and gatherings are often centered on shared meals and celebrations. Corsicans are noted for their great hospitality and eagerness to welcome tourists, making it simple to feel welcomed and involved in their tight-knit communities.

Another essential feature of Corsican traditions is respect for nature and the land. Corsicans have a strong connection to their natural environment, and methods like as sustainable farming, foraging, and fishing are practiced to ensure that the island's resources are preserved for future generations.

Corsican customs and traditions show the island's rich cultural past, tenacity, and profound connection to its land and people. Exploring these practices enables tourists to discover the colorful tapestry of Corsican traditions while delving into the core of Corsican identity.

Corsican Language

Corsican culture and identity are inextricably linked to the Corsican language, known as "Corsu" in the native dialect. It is a Romance language closely related to Italian, with influences from Tuscan and Ligurian dialects. Corsu is recognized as a regional language in Corsica and has official status alongside French.

The history of the Corsican language is extensive and intriguing. It has been spoken on the island for centuries, dating back to when Corsica was colonized by numerous civilizations such as the Etruscans, Greeks, Romans, and subsequently the Genoese.

Corsu is distinguished by its melodic and rhythmic quality, as well as specific sounds and intonations that set it apart from other Romance languages. The language is mostly spoken in rural regions, notably in the island's mountainous interior, where it has been better conserved through time.

Corsican identity and Corsican language preservation are inextricably linked. The language is a potent symbol of cultural history, and it has helped Corsicans develop a feeling of regional pride and solidarity. To preserve the continuation and transfer of Corsu to future generations, efforts have been undertaken to promote and renew its usage, especially in educational and cultural organizations.

While French is the official language of Corsica and is widely spoken across the island, the Corsican language may still be heard in daily life. It may be heard in local discussions, traditional melodies, and even on certain public signs. Many Corsicans are multilingual, and can easily switch between Corsu and French depending on the situation.

It may be beneficial for visitors visiting Corsica to acquire a few basic Corsican words and idioms. It shows respect for the local culture and may improve relationships with Corsicans, who typically appreciate the effort to connect with their language.

Overall, Corsican is a treasured element of the island's cultural fabric. Its continuous usage and preservation add to Corsica's distinctive character, showing the island's lasting spirit and tenacity.

Historical Background

Corsica has a rich and complex historical heritage that has defined its identity and affected its growth throughout the ages, thanks to its strategic position in the Mediterranean Sea. Corsica's history is woven with conquests, wars for independence, and cultural influences, ranging from ancient civilizations to numerous foreign dominions.

Ancient Civilizations

The earliest known occupants of Corsica were megalithic peoples who left behind spectacular stone constructions such as dolmens and menhirs. These prehistoric sites, which can be found all throughout the island, bore testament to a prehistoric past that stretches back thousands of years.

Greek immigrants from Phocaea built colonies on the eastern coast of Corsica in the sixth century BC, bringing their culture, language, and commerce with them. Their presence left an indelible mark on Corsican culture.

Roman rule

During the development of the Roman Republic in the second century BC, Corsica fell under Roman rule. The Romans built towns and fortresses, built highways, and formed Roman law and authority. Corsica's major centers were molded by Roman influence, which produced a period of relative peace and prosperity.

Foreign Dominance

Corsica had waves of foreign dominance in the centuries that followed. The island was governed by the Vandals, Ostrogoths, and Byzantines in turn. The entrance of the Lombards, a Germanic group from modern-day Italy, in the 8th century, however, had a lasting influence on Corsican civilization. The Lombards introduced feudalism to Corsica, establishing a feudal system that shaped the island's social and political structure for centuries.

Genoese Rule

The Republic of Genoa ruled over Corsica beginning in the 13th century. Genoa, a northern Italian naval power, attempted to capitalize on Corsica's strategic position and abundant resources. Genoese dominance lasted over five centuries and was characterized by intense opposition by Corsican chiefs fighting for independence.

Pasquale Paoli was a significant player in Corsica's war for independence. Paoli spearheaded a drive for Corsican autonomy in the 18th century, founding a democratic government and crafting a constitution that is often regarded as one of Europe's first modern constitutions. Although the campaign failed, Paoli's reputation as a Corsican national hero lives on.

French rule

In 1768, Genoa ceded Corsica to France under the Treaty of Versailles. Corsica became an official part of the French kingdom, and its fate became closely tied to that of France. When Napoleon Bonaparte, an Ajaccio native, rose to power and became Emperor of France during the French

Revolution, Corsica soared to prominence. Napoleon's effect on Corsica's history, as well as his ascension to worldwide importance, raised the island's stature even more.

Contemporary Corsica

Throughout the twentieth century, Corsica suffered political upheaval and independence movements. Separatist movements and battles between Corsican nationalists and the French authorities occurred on the island. However, in recent years, attempts have been undertaken within the framework of the French Republic to resolve issues and encourage more autonomy and cultural respect for Corsica.

Corsica now has a unique position as a geographical collectivity inside France, with its own regional administration and certain cultural and administrative autonomy. The island continues to embrace its own history and cultural heritage, drawing tourists drawn to its enthralling past.

Corsica's history is a story of subjugation, perseverance, and the desire of identity. The island's complicated past has affected its culture, language, and social fabric, resulting in an intriguing destination that combines old traditions with modern influences.

CHAPTER TWO
Planning your trip

Embarking on a journey to Corsica requires careful planning to ensure a smooth and hassle-free travel experience. Familiarizing yourself with the visa and travel requirements is essential to avoid any last-minute complications. Here is an overview of the necessary information regarding passports, visas, and entry requirements for different nationalities.

Best Time to Visit

When planning a vacation to Corsica, consider the optimum time to visit the island. Understanding weather trends, high tourist seasons, and off-season concerns will assist you in making an educated choice about when to begin on your Corsican journey.

Seasons and Weather

The climate of Corsica is Mediterranean, with moderate winters and scorching summers. Every year, the island receives over 300 days of sunlight, making it an ideal destination for both outdoor enthusiasts and sun lovers.

Corsica is very beautiful in the spring (March to May). Temperatures in the range of 15°C to 20°C (59°F to 68°F) are normally nice. As flowers blossom and the landscape comes alive, the island erupts into bright hues. Spring also has the benefit of fewer visitors and reduced lodging expenses.

Summer (June to August) is Corsica's busiest tourism season. The island has pleasant temperatures that range from 25°C to 30°C (77°F to 86°F), with occasional highs in the 30s (86°F+). The coastal regions are ideal for beach activities, swimming, and participating in water sports. It is crucial to remember, however, that famous tourist destinations might get congested during this period, and hotel and airfare tickets tend to be higher.

Autumn temperatures range from 18°C to 25°C (64°F to 77°F) from September through November. The island is less crowded than in the summer, giving it an ideal time to discover Corsica's natural beauty, go trekking, and enjoy outdoor sports. The water stays warm, while the scenery changes to beautiful fall hues.

Corsica's low season lasts from December to February. While temperatures on the island range from 8°C to 15°C (46°F to 59°F), it still has a temperate climate when compared to many other European locations. Winter is an excellent season to visit Corsica's medieval villages and cities since the weather is milder and you can enjoy local customs and festivities.

Peak Travel Seasons

Corsica's busiest tourist months are the summer months, from June to August. This is when the island sees the most tourists, particularly beachgoers and sunbathers. Popular seaside places, such as Porto-Vecchio and Calvi, might get congested around this season, so plan ahead of time for lodgings and activities.

Corsica also sees an inflow of visitors around Easter and other big public holidays, when many people take advantage of long vacations to visit the island. When planning your vacation, keep these peak times in mind, particularly if you prefer a calmer and less crowded experience.

Considerations for the Off-Season

There are benefits to visiting Corsica during the off-season. The island sees fewer people from late October to early spring, providing a more calm and genuine experience. You may appreciate Corsica's natural beauty without crowds, visit old towns at your leisure, and interact with people on a deeper level.

During the off-season, you may discover more economical lodging alternatives and more freedom in designing your schedule. It is important to note, however, that certain attractions, tourist services, and beach amenities may have restricted availability or working hours during this period. It's always a good idea to plan ahead of time.

Finally, the ideal time to visit Corsica is determined by your particular interests, whether you favor lively summer beach days or peaceful off-season exploration. Consider the weather, tourist seasons, and your intended experiences when determining the best time to visit Corsica.

Visa and Travel Requirements

Visa and Travel Requirements

Travelers entering Corsica, a French territory, must follow France's visa and entrance regulations. Because Corsica is part of France, the same restrictions apply when visiting the island.

Passport

To enter Corsica, all tourists, regardless of nationality, must have a valid passport. Make sure your passport is valid for at least six months after your departure date from Corsica. It is best to create a duplicate of your passport and store it apart from the original in case of emergency.

Visa

France is a participant of the Schengen Agreement, which permits citizens of several countries to travel visa-free for up to 90 days during a 180-day period. If you are a citizen of a Schengen member nation, such as the United States, Canada, or Australia, you do not need a visa for up to 90 days. However, it is essential to check the individual visa restrictions for your place of origin, since certain nationalities may need a visa even for short stays.

Entry Requirements for Different Nationalities

The entry requirements for Corsica vary based on your nationality. Here are a few scenarios to consider

Citizens of Schengen Member Countries: If you are a citizen of a Schengen member country, you may visit Corsica without a visa if you have a valid passport or national identification card. This includes citizens of the European Union (EU), Iceland, Liechtenstein, Norway, and Switzerland.

Citizens of non-Schengen member countries: Such as the United States, Canada, Australia, and many others, may normally visit Corsica without a visa for stays of up to 90 days within a 180-day period. However, it is important to check the visa requirements for your nationality before flying.

Non-European Union (EU) Citizens: If you are a non-EU citizen from India, China, or Russia, you may need a Schengen visa to visit Corsica. To learn the visa requirements and procedure, contact the French Embassy or Consulate in your native country.

It is essential to remember that visa laws are subject to change, so it is best to check with the appropriate consular services or official government websites for the most up-to-date and correct information on passport, visa, and entrance requirements.

Furthermore, having travel insurance that covers medical bills and trip cancellations is suggested, since unexpected events may develop during your travels.

You can assure a smooth entrance into Corsica and enjoy your visit on this gorgeous island by learning the visa and travel requirements. Proper preparation and adherence to the appropriate requirements will provide the groundwork for a wonderful and stress-free trip to Corsica.

Accommodation Options

When planning a vacation to Corsica, it is essential to evaluate your lodging alternatives in order to have a comfortable and pleasurable stay on the island. Corsica has a wide choice of lodgings to suit a variety of tastes and budgets. Corsica's primary forms of lodging are as follows:

Hotels

Hotels: Corsica has a diverse range of hotels, ranging from budget-friendly to luxurious alternatives. Hotels may be found in large cities like as Bastia, Ajaccio, Calvi, and Porto-Vecchio, as well as in smaller villages and along the coast. Corsica's hotels often reflect the island's distinct character, with many having beautiful sea views, closeness to the beach, or mountain panoramas. Whether you're looking for a boutique hotel, a family-friendly resort, or a spa getaway, Corsica provides lots of possibilities.

Hôtel & Spa des Pêcheurs (Bonifacio)

- The hotel is located in Bonifacio gives guests convenient access to the town's historic core, where they can tour the medieval fortress, meander through lovely little lanes, and take in panoramic views from the cliffside.

- Bonifacio is well-known for its colorful marina, which offers boat excursions, yacht rentals, and water sports including as sailing, snorkeling, and diving.

- The Michelin-starred restaurant of Hôtel & Spa des Pêcheurs highlights the gastronomic joys of the island, blending fresh seafood, locally produced products, and inventive tastes. It provides an unforgettable dining experience, focusing on gourmet Mediterranean food.

Hotel Misincu (Cagnano)

Cagnano lies in the Cap Corse area, which is famed for its rough coastline, quiet beaches, and lovely fishing towns. Exploring this region provides guests with the opportunity to experience the true Corsican way of life.

- The hotel's own beach offers a tranquil and intimate location for sunbathing and relaxation. Water sports like as paddleboarding, kayaking, and seaside yoga sessions are also available to guests.

- The spa at Hotel Misincu provides a refuge for relaxation and regeneration with a variety of holistic treatments inspired by Corsican traditions and natural materials.

Hotel La Villa (Calvi)

- Calvi is a vibrant seaside town with a large sandy beach and a well-preserved fortress. Visitors may wander the cobblestone alleyways of the citadel, see the Cathedral of Saint John the Baptist, and enjoy the lively ambiance of the town's restaurants and bars.

- Because of the hotel's closeness to the beach, guests may easily enjoy sunbathing, swimming, and water sports. Calvi Beach is well-known for its golden beaches and stunning blue waves.

- The spa at Hotel La Villa provides a variety of treatments and therapies to assist visitors relax and revitalize. Guests may luxuriate in a serene haven of relaxation with massages and facials, as well as hydrotherapy and wellness rituals.

Tourists may acquire a better idea of the distinctive attractions and experiences that each hotel and its surrounding locations provide by offering these extra facts. This information allows customers to make educated selections and personalize their stay in Corsica to their own tastes and interests.

Resorts
Hotel La Plage Casadelmar (Porto-Vecchio)
- **Location**: Located in Porto-Vecchio on Corsica's southeastern coast, this magnificent resort has a fantastic beachfront setting. It's close to the town center, so it's simple to go to stores, restaurants, and other attractions.

- Special Features: Hotel La Plage Casadelmar has modern and stylishly constructed rooms and suites, many of which have own patios or balconies with stunning views of Porto-Vecchio Bay. The resort has its own beach area where visitors may relax on sun loungers and enjoy the virgin sandy coastlines. The outdoor pool is a refreshing retreat, and the on-site gourmet restaurant offers a gastronomic experience featuring Corsican and Mediterranean cuisines.

The cost of a night at Hotel La Plage Casadelmar begins about €400 (EUR) and varies according on the hotel type, season, and availability.

Les Bergeries de Palombaggia (Porto-Vecchio)

- location: This beautiful resort is nestled in a calm location near Palombaggia Beach, only a short drive from Porto-Vecchio. It enables visitors to enjoy the natural beauty of the famed Palombaggia coastline while being close to the town's facilities.

Les Bergeries de Palombaggia provides separate villas with a rustic but refined environment. The resort is surrounded by beautiful grounds, providing a relaxing ambience. Guests may relax by the outdoor pool, sunbathe on luxurious lounge chairs, and eat at the on-site restaurant, which serves regional cuisine. The attentive service and modest environment of the resort make it a great alternative for anyone looking for a calm escape.

The cost per night at Les Bergeries de Palombaggia begins about €300 (EUR) and varies according to the cottage type, season, and availability.

U Capu Biancu (Bonifacio – Location

U Capu Biancu is perched on a cliff overlooking the Mediterranean Sea near Bonifacio in southern Corsica. Its hilltop location provides breathtaking panoramic views of the turquoise ocean and shoreline, making for a really spectacular setting.

- Special Features: U Capu Biancu offers well-appointed rooms and suites, some with their own patios or balconies overlooking the sea. The resort has direct access to a private beach where guests may relax on loungers and soak up the rays. The infinity pool provides a calm setting for swimming and admiring the breathtaking views. Guests may enjoy restorative spa treatments and exquisite meals at the on-site restaurant, which features Corsican delicacies.

The cost of a night at U Capu Biancu begins about €350 (EUR), and varies based on the room type, season, and availability.

Please keep in mind that the prices shown are estimates and may vary depending on seasonality, accommodation type, and any extra services or packages you pick. For the most current and up-to-date price information, always check with the resorts directly or via reputable booking channels.

Bed & Breakfast
Casa Theodora (Nonza)

- Location: Casa Theodora is located in the lovely town of Nonza, on Corsica's west coast. This charming town provides a calm and attractive location for a relaxing break, with spectacular views of the sea and surrounding countryside.

- Approximate Cost: Depending on the season and availability, a double room at Casa Theodora costs roughly €120 (EUR) each night.

Casa Theodora is a beautiful stone structure that has been meticulously repaired and transformed into a charming Bed & Breakfast. Each room is uniquely designed in a delightful rustic manner, resulting in a warm and inviting ambiance. Guests may enjoy a great breakfast provided on the terrace, which overlooks the sea and is the ideal place to begin the day. The B&B also has a nice garden where visitors may relax and enjoy the peace and quiet of the surroundings.

L'Auberge du Prunelli (Tavaco)

- Location: L'Auberge du Prunelli is situated in the town of Tavaco, which is a short drive from Ajaccio, Corsica's capital. The B&B is surrounded by rich foliage and breathtaking mountains, making for a tranquil and picturesque setting for a pleasant stay.

- Approximate Cost: Depending on the season and availability, a double room at L'Auberge du Prunelli costs roughly €90 (EUR) each night.

L'Auberge du Prunelli is located in a classic Corsican stone building that exudes beauty and character. The rooms are warm and comfortable, with a rustic environment that represents the local character. Guests may enjoy a delectable breakfast, which includes handmade pastries and jams, adding a personal touch to the experience. The B&B also has a lovely patio and garden where visitors may relax, breathe in fresh air, and admire the natural surroundings.

Casa Capellini (Santa Reparata di Balagna)

- Location: Casa Capellini is located in the picturesque Balagne area of Corsica, near the town of Santa Reparata di Balagna. The B&B is well located for visiting the neighboring sandy beaches and the picturesque town of Ile-Rousse, providing the ideal combination of rest and discovery.

- Approximate Cost: Depending on the season and availability, a double room at Casa Capellini costs roughly €100 (EUR) per night.

- Unique Features: Casa Capellini is located in a classic Corsican stone mansion that showcases true Corsican architecture. The apartments are elegantly designed, combining comfort and elegance. Guests may enjoy a great breakfast served on the patio, which offers breathtaking views of the hamlet and surrounding mountains. After a day of exploring, visitors may repose in the B&B's pleasant lounge room, where they can recline, read a book, or just decompress.

These Corsican Bed & Breakfasts provide a one-of-a-kind and customized experience that allows tourists to immerse themselves in the local culture and hospitality. The prices shown are estimates and may vary depending on variables such as accommodation type, season, and availability. For the most current and up-to-date information, contact the businesses directly or visit their official websites.

Budget-friendly accommodations
Camping Les Oliviers (Porto-Vecchio)
Camping Les Oliviers is situated in Porto-Vecchio, a prominent Corsican coastal town noted for its magnificent beaches and lively atmosphere.

- **Price**: A camping site or a modest accommodation unit at Camping Les Oliviers costs roughly €20-€30 (EUR) per night,

43

making it an attractive alternative for budget-conscious vacationers.

- **Special Features**: This campground has a variety of amenities, including shaded tent and caravan spaces, as well as modest mobile homes or bungalows. Among the facilities available to guests are sanitation blocks, a common cooking area, and a swimming pool. Camping Les Oliviers is a fantastic alternative for nature enthusiasts and those looking for a low-cost way to appreciate the beauty of Corsica.

Hotel du Nord (Bastia)

- Location: The Hotel du Nord is in Bastia, a dynamic city in northern Corsica noted for its picturesque old town, thriving harbor, and cultural attractions.

- **Price**: A regular room at Hotel du Nord costs roughly €50-€70 (EUR) per night, making it an attractive option for budget tourists.

- **Unique Features:** Hotel du Nord provides pleasant rooms with necessary facilities such as private bathrooms, free Wi-Fi, and satellite TV. The hotel is perfectly positioned in the city center, making it easy for travelers to visit local attractions, shops, and restaurants. With its low prices and central location, Hotel du Nord is a handy and cost-effective solution for visitors to Bastia.

Auberge A Pignata (Zonza)

- **Location**: Auberge A Pignata is located in the town of Zonza, in the heart of Corsica's magnificent mountainous area known as the Alta Rocca.

- **Price**: Regular accommodation at Auberge A Pignata costs roughly €60-€80 (EUR) per night, making it a reasonable option for travelers wishing to experience the natural beauty of the Alta Rocca area.

- **Special Features**: This lovely inn offers pleasant and warm rooms with en-suite bathrooms. Guests may dine in the on-site restaurant, which provides great Corsican cuisine, and unwind on the outdoor patio, which overlooks the mountains. Auberge A Pignata is a low-cost choice for visitors looking for a tranquil and genuine experience in Corsica's hilly area.

These low-cost lodgings provide pleasant and economical choices for those wishing to discover Corsica on a budget. To guarantee the most accurate and up-to-date information for your selected vacation dates, verify availability and exact price directly with the establishments or via trustworthy booking platforms.

Camping and RV Parks
Here are three Corsican camping and RV parks, together with their locations, particular features, estimated expenses, and vital safety precautions:

Camping Arinella Bianca (Ghisonaccia)
- **Location**: Ghisonaccia, on Corsica's eastern coast. It is surrounded by beautiful Mediterranean flora and provides direct access to a magnificent white sandy beach.

- **Special Features**: Camping Arinella Bianca has a large tent, campervan, and RV spaces, as well as luxurious mobile homes and bungalows for rent. It has sanitary blocks, a grocery shop, a restaurant, a swimming pool, sports courts, and a children's club. The campground hosts a variety of activities and entertainment events.

- **Cost**: A camping space costs roughly €20 per night while renting a mobile home or cottage might cost between €60 and €150 per night, depending on the season and kind of accommodation.

- **Precautions**: Obey the campsite's fire safety standards, respect the environment, and keep your valuables secure. Learn the swimming pool guidelines and supervise children accordingly.

Camping U Pezzo (Bonifacio)
- **Location**: In southern Corsica, near Bonifacio, surrounded by tranquil farmland and close to the spectacular cliffs and beaches of Bonifacio.

- **Unique Features**: Camping U Pezzo has large plots for tents, campervans, and RVs. It has contemporary restrooms, a swimming pool, a bar, and a restaurant offering local cuisine. The campground also provides entertainment and activities for people of all ages.

- **Price**: The cost of a camping spot ranges from €15 to €25 per night, depending on the season and pitch size.

- **Precautions**: Make sure your items are secure, observe the camping regulations, and appreciate the peace and quiet of the surrounding countryside.

Camping Les Ilots d'Or (Santa-Lucia-di-Moriani)
Santa-Lucia-di-Moriani is located on Corsica's eastern coast, among magnificent sandy beaches and surrounded by mountains and woods.

- **Unique Features**: Camping Les Ilots d'Or offers large and shaded tssss, campervan, and RV spaces. It has contemporary sanitary facilities, a swimming pool, a restaurant, a grocery shop, and a playground for children. The campground conducts a variety of sports and entertainment events.

- **Price**: Depending on the season and pitch size, the cost of a camping spot ranges from €20 to €30 a night.

- **Precautions**: Follow the campsite's safety standards, appropriately dispose of garbage, and be environmentally conscious.

When staying in a campground or RV park, it is important to follow the laws and regulations of the campground, practice proper hygiene, and be respectful to other campers. Furthermore, for the most accurate and up-to-date information, always confirm the availability, particular facilities, and price directly with the camping parks or via trustworthy booking sites.

Currency and Banking
Currency Exchange
As a first-time visitor to Corsica, you should be aware of your currency exchange alternatives. Corsica, like the rest of France, uses the Euro (€) as its official currency. It is recommended that you convert your money into Euros before to your travel. This is something you may accomplish at your local bank or currency exchange office. It is suggested that you examine exchange rates and fees to get the most bang for your buck.

While currency conversion facilities are accessible in Corsica's main cities and tourist destinations, it's a good idea to carry some Euros in cash when visiting more isolated places or smaller enterprises that may not take card payments.

ATMs and Banking Services

ATMs may be found across Corsica, particularly in larger towns and cities. They provide an easy option to withdraw cash in Euros using a debit or credit card Look for ATMs associated with reputable banks, which are usually found in well-lit and busy areas. Inform your bank or credit card company about your trip to Corsica well in advance. This step assures that your cards will not be banned when used overseas due to suspicious activities. It's also a good idea to have a backup card in case your main card fails.

Corsica boasts a variety of financial services, including currency exchange, money transfers, and traveler's cheques, in addition to ATMs. Banks are usually open Monday through Friday during normal business hours, with some branches being operating on Saturday mornings. Larger towns and cities have several banking alternatives, but smaller villages may have fewer.

Precautions: When using ATMs or performing card transactions, prioritize your safety and protect yourself from possible fraud. Here are a few measures to take:

1. Only use ATMs in well-lit and safe settings, such as bank premises or busy streets.

2. When entering your PIN, shield it to prevent others from viewing or capturing it.

3. Check your bank statements or online banking on a regular basis for any illegal activities and report any suspicious behavior to your bank right away.

4. Keep a variety of payment alternatives on hand, including cash and credit cards, for flexibility and ease.

By taking these steps and knowing currency exchange and banking services in Corsica, you may assure a pleasant and safe financial experience as a first-time visitor.

Language and Communication
Corsican Language Basics

The Corsican language holds a significant cultural and historical value in Corsica. It is a Romance language that shares similarities with Italian and French, reflecting the island's unique cultural heritage. While the official language of Corsica is French, Corsican is still spoken by a significant portion of the population, particularly in rural areas and smaller towns.

Here are a few basic Corsican language phrases that can be useful during your visit:

- Hello: Bonghjornu (bon-jor-nu)

- Goodbye: Basta (bas-ta)

- Thank you: Grazia (gra-tsi-a)

- Please: Per piacè (per pia-che)

- Yes: Si (see)

- No: No (no)

Learning a few Corsican phrases can enhance your cultural experience and show respect for the local traditions. However, it's important to note that most Corsicans also speak French and may understand basic English, especially in tourist areas.

English and Other Widely Spoken Languages
In Corsica, French is the primary language of communication. As a popular tourist destination, many locals in Corsica, especially those working in the tourism industry, have a good understanding of English. In major tourist areas, you can expect to find people who can communicate in English, making it easier to navigate through your travel experience.

It's always helpful to learn a few essential French phrases, as it will greatly assist you in everyday interactions. Here are some common phrases:

- Hello: Bonjour (bon-zhur)

- Goodbye: Au revoir (o rev-wahr)

- Thank you: Merci (mer-see)

- Please: S'il vous plaît (seel-voo-pleh)

- Excuse me: Excusez-moi (ex-koo-zay mwa)

- Do you speak English?: Parlez-vous anglais? (par-lay-voo on-glay)

Aside from French and English, Italian is another language that can be heard in certain areas of Corsica, especially along the eastern coast due to its proximity to Italy. However, English and French are the most widely spoken languages and will generally suffice for communication with locals and accessing essential services.

Having a basic understanding of these languages or carrying a phrasebook or translation app can greatly facilitate your interactions and make your travel experience in Corsica more enjoyable and engaging.

How to Get to Corsica

Corsica, a lovely Mediterranean island, has a variety of transportation alternatives to reach its coastlines. Corsica is well-connected and readily accessible, whether you like to travel by air, boat, or public transit.

By air

Corsica is served by four main airports, which provide both local and international flights:

1. **Bastia-Poretta Airport (BIA)**: Located near Bastia on the island's northeastern coast, Bastia-Poretta Airport is one of Corsica's busiest airports. With frequent flights to and from major towns in France, Italy, and other European countries, it serves as the main entrance to the island.

2. **Ajaccio-Napoleon Bonaparte Airport (AJA):** Located in Ajaccio, Corsica's city, Ajaccio-Napoleon Bonaparte Airport provides local and international flights. It is a handy entrance point for visitors from mainland France and other European nations.

3. Calvi-Sainte-Catherine Airport (CLY): Located in Calvi on Corsica's northwestern coast, Calvi-Sainte-Catherine Airport is a popular option for travelers to the Balagne area. It

conducts both internal and international flights, linking Corsica to towns around Europe.

4. Figari-Sud Corse airfield (FSC): Located at Figari in Corsica's southernmost region, Figari-Sud Corse Airport is an important airfield on the island. It provides internal and international flights, providing links to key French and European cities.

These airports are well-equipped with amenities and services like as car rental desks, cafés, stores, and transit alternatives to city centers and other island locations.

Domestic and International Airlines

Several airlines provide frequent flights to Corsica, making it easy for travelers to get there. Corsica is served by the following major airlines:

- **Air France**: Air France operates domestic flights to Corsica from cities around mainland France, including Paris, Lyon, Marseille, and Nice. They also provide international flights to Corsica from other European cities.

- **Air Corsica**: As Corsica's regional airline, Air Corsica is critical in linking the island to mainland France and other European nations. They provide regular flights to and from Corsica's main airports, which include Bastia, Ajaccio, Calvi, and Figari.

- **Ryanair**: Ryanair, a low-cost airline, flies to Corsica from a number of European locations. They provide reasonable solutions for customers looking for low-cost plane travel to the island.

- **EasyJet**: Another prominent low-cost airline that conducts flights to Corsica from numerous European locations, giving travellers with easy and economical travel alternatives.

Check with these airlines on reputable travel websites for the most up-to-date flight schedules, rates, and availability depending on your trip dates and desired departure airport.

Ferries and Ports
Ferry Routes and Operators

Traveling to Corsica via boat is a good alternative if you want a gorgeous maritime voyage. Corsica is well-connected by ferry lines to mainland France, Italy, and other Mediterranean locations. The boat voyage provides stunning views of the coastline as well as a calm travel experience Several ferry operators provide services to Corsica, including

- **Corsica Ferries**: Corsica Ferries is a significant ferry company that connects Corsica to several ports in France and Italy. They provide passenger and car transportation, as well as overnight trips and high-speed ferry services.

- **La Méridionale**: La Méridionale Ridionale conducts ferry services between Corsica and mainland France, mostly between the ports of Marseille and Toulon. They provide both passenger and vehicle travel.

- **Moby Lines**: Moby Lines is another ferry company that connects Corsica to mainland France and Italy. They provide a variety of services, including overnight crossings and amenities like cabins, restaurants, and entertainment venues.

Ports of Entry in Corsica

Corsica has a number of ports of entry that handle ferry arrivals and departures. Among the important ports are:

- **Port of Bastia**: The Port of Bastia, located at Bastia on Corsica's northeastern coast, is one of the busiest ports on the island. It is an important ferry connecting point, with several services to and from mainland France and Italy.

- **Port of Ajaccio**: Located in Ajaccio, Corsica's capital, the Port of Ajaccio offers ferry services that link the island to mainland France and other Mediterranean locations.

- **Port of Calvi**: Located on the northwestern coast of Corsica, the Port of Calvi acts as a gateway for ferry connections to mainland France and Italy.

- **Porto-Vecchio**: Located in Porto-Vecchio, Corsica's southeast, the Porto-Vecchio provides ferry services linking Corsica to mainland France and other Mediterranean ports.

Parking lots, passenger terminals, and amenities such as cafés, stores, and car rental offices are available at these ports.

Corsican Public Transportation
Coaches and buses

Corsica has an extensive bus network that links the island's municipalities, villages, and tourist spots. Several businesses, notably the Regional Transport Authority (CORSICA BUS), manage the bus system, which provides easy transit alternatives for touring Corsica.

The buses are comfortable and well-equipped, guaranteeing a pleasant journey. Bus schedules and routes are easily accessible at bus stops, tourist information centers, and online. It is best to double-check the schedules ahead of time, since they may change depending on the season.

Train Services

The Corsican Railways (CFC) operates a picturesque narrow-gauge train network on Corsica. The trains go throughout the island, providing stunning views of the landscape and shoreline. The train network connects major towns and cities, making it a suitable form of transportation for visiting the interior areas of Corsica.

The CFC runs many railway lines, notably the Main Line (Linea Principale), which links Bastia to Ajaccio via Corte, and the Balagne Line (Linea di Balagna), which connects Calvi to L'Île-Rousse. The trains are pleasant, and timetables are accessible at railway stations, tourist information centers, and online.

Taxis and Car Rentals

Taxis are abundant in Corsica, notably at airports, ferry terminals, and large cities. They provide a quick and dependable mode of transportation, whether you want a short journey or a transfer to a specified location. Before beginning the trip, it is important to confirm the fare with the driver.

Car rental services are particularly popular in Corsica, allowing you to explore the island at your own speed. Major automobile rental businesses have locations at airports, ferry terminals, and throughout cities. To assure availability, it is best to reserve a rental vehicle ahead of time, particularly during high travel seasons.

To summarize, traveling to Corsica is quite simple, thanks to a variety of transportation choices. Corsica has a well-connected and accessible transportation system, whether you fly into one of the main airports, take a boat from France or Italy, or tour the island via public transit. You may pick the finest means of transportation for your Corsican vacation by preparing ahead of time and evaluating your interests.

CHAPTER THREE
Exploring the Regions of Corsica
Ajaccio and the West Coast

The Ajaccio area and Corsica's beautiful West Coast are known for their natural beauty, rich historical legacy, and vibrant metropolitan culture. This book will take you on an in-depth tour of Ajaccio, Corsica's capital city, and its outstanding attractions, providing a memorable experience in this charming corner of the Mediterranean.

Ajaccio City Guide

Ajaccio, located on Corsica's gorgeous West Coast, provides a riveting combination of history, culture, and breathtaking surroundings. Here's a full breakdown of everything you may expect to find in Ajaccio:

Maison Bonaparte

- Travel back in time by visiting the Maison Bonaparte, Napoleon Bonaparte's ancestral house.

- Immerse yourself in the museum's intriguing exhibitions, which provide a detailed insight into the life and legacy of the great military and political leader.

- Take in the restored furniture, souvenirs, and personal objects that provide a look into the history of the Bonaparte family.

Ajaccio Cathedral

- Visit the Ajaccio Cathedral, an amazing ecclesiastical structure that serves as the Bonaparte family's ultimate resting place.

- Take around the spectacular architecture, including Napoleon's parents' marble monument, Charles and Letizia Bonaparte.

- Take a minute to relax and explore the magnificent interior, which is filled with elaborate religious artwork.

Citadel of Ajaccio

- Climb to the Citadel of Ajaccio, an ancient castle built on a hill with sweeping views of the city and the turquoise Mediterranean Sea.

- Capture spectacular panoramic vistas of the city's shoreline, busy port, and beautiful mountains.

- Wander inside the citadel's old walls, bastions, and watchtowers to learn about its fascinating history.

The Fesch Museum

- Enter the world of art at the Fesch Museum, which has one of the most important collections of Italian paintings outside of Italy.

- Explore the numerous galleries and admire works by great painters such as Botticelli, Titian, and Veronese.

- Take in the broad array of artworks on show, which includes religious icons, portraits, landscapes.

Local shopping districts and markets

- Immerse yourself in the colorful local culture by visiting Ajaccio's busy markets, such as Place Foch.

- Savor the tastes of Corsica by eating regional specialties such as handmade cheeses, charcuterie, and fragrant honey.

- Browse the beautiful boutiques and artisan stores that line the streets, providing one-of-a-kind souvenirs, local crafts, and traditional Corsican items.

Ajaccio's rich tradition, cultural riches, and inviting attitude make it a must-see destination on Corsica's West Coast. Ajaccio guarantees a remarkable experience for every guest with its historical importance, natural beauty, and cultural attractions.

Sanguinaires Islands

The Sanguinaires Islands, a collection of four tiny islands only a few kilometers off the coast of Ajaccio, are a genuine jewel of the Corsican coastline. These islands, noted for their extraordinary natural beauty, provide a welcome respite from the hustle and bustle of city life. What you should anticipate finding in the Sanguinaires Islands is as follows:

1. The Sanguinaires Islands are known for their beautiful beaches and crystal-clear blue seas. Whether you want to rest in solitude or seek adventure by snorkeling or swimming, these beaches provide a tranquil and scenic backdrop.

2. Rugged Cliffs and Coastal Scenery: The spectacular cliffs that border the shoreline will capture you as you explore the Sanguinaires Islands. The craggy topography contrasts well with the deep blue water, providing a wonderfully lovely view.

3. Enchanting Sunsets: The Sanguinaires Islands are noted for their breathtaking sunsets. The sky morphs into a kaleidoscope of warm colors as the sun sets, throwing a golden light over the islands and creating a wonderful

ambiance. Seeing the sunset from one of the islands is a once-in-a-lifetime event.

4. Boat Tours: Consider taking a boat trip to properly enjoy the splendor of the Sanguinaires Islands. These cruises provide a unique view of the islands, enabling you to explore their rocky cliffs, secluded coves, and marine life. Some trips also include swimming and snorkeling in the beautiful seas that surround the islands.

5. Hiking paths: For those who prefer outdoor activities, the Sanguinaires Islands include a number of hiking paths that take you through their natural landscapes. Trek through Mediterranean greenery on well-marked routes that provide panoramic views of the coastline and nearby islands.

6. Wildlife Spotting: The Sanguinaires Islands are a wildlife enthusiast's paradise. Keep a look out for seabirds such as cormorants and seagulls as they fly through the air or sit on the cliffs. You could even see seals sunbathing in the sun on the rocky shoreline if you're fortunate.

The Sanguinaires Islands are a real natural marvel, providing a peaceful and scenic retreat. A visit to these islands is guaranteed to leave you with lasting memories of Corsica's coastline beauty, whether you want to relax on the pristine beaches, go on a boat excursion, explore hiking paths, or just absorb the breathtaking sunsets.

Gulf Valinco

The Gulf of Valinco, situated on Corsica's gorgeous west coast, is a compelling location rich in natural beauty, lovely cities, and intriguing historical buildings. Here's a more in-depth look at the popular sites and activities in this gorgeous area:

Propriano

Propriano is a charming seaside village on the Gulf of Valinco. Its primary draw is its stunning sandy beaches, such as Plage du Lido and Plage de Mancinu, where you can relax, tan, and enjoy the cool Mediterranean waves. The town's beachfront promenade is lined with cafés, restaurants, and stores, providing a vibrant ambiance as well as the chance to sample wonderful local food and buy gifts. Water sports aficionados will have enough to do here, with snorkeling, scuba diving, jet skiing, and sailing available.

Campomoro

The charming town of Campomoro, nestled in the Gulf of Valinco, appeals with its stunning splendor and calm environment. Campomoro's gorgeous beach, with soft golden sand and crystal-clear blue seas, is its main draw. Relax on the beach, go for a leisurely swim, or go snorkeling to discover the underwater world. The famous Genoese tower, which rises above the settlement, is a historic landmark that provides panoramic views of the shoreline and surrounding environment. Don't pass up the opportunity to wander along the coastline paths and take in the spectacular views.

Porto Pollo

Water sports aficionados, mainly windsurfers and kite surfers, flock to Porto Pollo. Because of its great position and perfect wind conditions, it is an ideal spot for adrenaline-pumping water experiences. You'll find superb facilities, equipment rentals, and even lessons to help you make the most of your time on the waves, whether you're a seasoned veteran or a novice. The beach itself is a lovely expanse of sand, ideal for sunbathing, picnics, and taking in the relaxed seaside vibe.

Filitosa

Exploration of the ancient site of Filitosa, an archaeological gem situated in the Gulf of Valinco, will transport you back in time. This incredible site has ancient megaliths and ruins dating back thousands of years. Take a guided walk to learn about the site's history and importance, as well as the mysterious stone sculptures known as "menhirs." These menhirs, carved with complex human forms, provide an intriguing peek into the past. The location also has a museum where visitors may learn more about the island's historic history.

The Gulf of Valinco combines natural beauty, cultural heritage, and recreational attractions. This location provides something for everyone, whether you want to relax on sandy beaches, participate in exhilarating water sports, or learn about the island's history. Immerse yourself in the splendor of the Gulf of Valinco and make long-lasting memories of your stay to this beautiful stretch of Corsica's west coast.

Bastia City

Bastia and the North Coast

The Bastia area and Corsica's North Coast provide a remarkable combination of history, natural beauty, and bustling coastal villages. Let's have a look at the features of this beautiful area:

Bastia, the capital of northern Corsica, is a picturesque harbor town that serves as the island's entrance. Here's a full breakdown of everything you can find in Bastia:

- **Vieux Port**: Begin your trip in the magnificent Vieux Port, Bastia's historic center. Stroll down the waterfront promenade, which is adorned with brightly colored buildings, busy cafés, and restaurants serving excellent local food. Don't pass up the chance to eat fresh seafood meals while taking in views of the waterfront.

- **Terra Nova**: Travel to the Terra Nova neighborhood to see the majestic Citadel of Bastia. This well-preserved stronghold provides panoramic views of the city and the sea. Explore its old fortifications, the Governor's Palace, and the region's history and traditions.

- **Saint-Nicolas Square**: Immerse yourself in the local atmosphere in Saint-Nicolas Square, a lively gathering spot for both residents and tourists. Spend some time people-watching, sipping coffee at a sidewalk café, and browsing the neighboring stores and boutiques.

- **Place du Marché**: At Place du Marché, you may experience the vivid atmosphere of the daily market. You may immerse yourself in the sights, sounds, and smells of Corsica right here. Explore the vendors selling fresh fruit, cheeses, charcuterie, and regional delicacies. Engage in conversation with the friendly merchants and try some of the island's gastronomic delicacies.

Cap Corse Peninsula

The Cap Corse Peninsula, situated north of Bastia, is a rough and scenic area with beautiful scenery and charming settlements. Here are some of the highlights of this region:

- **Macinaggio**: Begin your tour in Macinaggio, a lovely beach hamlet and the entryway to Cap Corse. Explore the marina, walk along the sandy beach, and dine at one of the waterfront restaurants.

- **Erbalunga**: Visit Erbalunga, which is famed for its picturesque fishing port and lovely alleys. Admire the Genoese tower, peruse art galleries exhibiting local talent, and dine at one of the classic eateries.

- **Sentier des Douaniers**: Take a walk along the Sentier des Douaniers (Customs Path), a seaside route that snakes around the cliffs of the peninsula and provides beautiful views of the Mediterranean Sea. Hike across maquis-covered hills, find secret coves, and take in the natural beauty of the coast.

Nebbio Region

The Nebbio region, situated in northwest Corsica, is noted for its vineyards, olive orchards, and lovely towns. Here are some of the picturesque region's highlights:

- **Patrimonio**: Visit the hamlet of Patrimonio, which is known for its vineyards and world-class wines. Visit local vineyards to sample the delectable Niellucciu and Vermentinu wines and learn about Corsican winemaking traditions.

- **Saint-Florent:** Explore this charming village set between the mountains and the sea. Explore the picturesque alleyways, see the Genoese fortress, and relax on the sandy beaches. Don't pass up the opportunity to experience local food at one of the seaside eateries.

- **Desert des Agriates**: Explore the rough wildness of the Desert des Agriates, a natural reserve noted for its pristine vistas and raw beauty.

Enjoy the sense of being immersed in nature as you explore the undulating hills, secret beaches, and dunes.

Exploring ancient cities and strongholds, trekking along spectacular coasts, and enjoying in local culinary delights are just a few of the activities available in the Bastia and North Coast area of Corsica. Immerse yourself in the beauty and rich tradition of this enthralling region of the island, and make lasting memories of your Corsican journey.

Balagne and Calvi

Corsica's Calvi and Balagne area is known for its beautiful scenery, charming seaside towns, and rich cultural legacy. Let's go into the specifics of this fascinating area:

Calvi City Guide

Calvi, a lovely village on Corsica's northwest coast, provides an ideal combination of history, natural beauty, and a dynamic beach lifestyle. Here's a detailed guide to explore Calvi:

- **Citadel of Calvi**: Begin your adventure in the Citadel, the ancient center of Calvi. This well-preserved stronghold provides panoramic views of the town and the Mediterranean's azure waves. Explore its meandering lanes, pay a visit to the Cathedral of Saint John the Baptist, and immerse yourself in the medieval atmosphere.

- **Calvi Marina:** Take a walk through the marina, which is dotted with colorful yachts and attractive eateries. Dine at one of the seaside eateries, enjoy fresh seafood, and soak in the laid-back vibe.

- **Calvi Beach**: Unwind on Calvi Beach, a beautiful length of beach with crystal-clear seas and a background of jagged mountains. Spend your days relaxing, sunbathing, swimming, or participating in water activities such as snorkeling, kayaking, or paddleboarding.

- **Rue Clemenceau**: Stroll through the main street of Calvi, which is dotted with stores, boutiques, and cafés. Browse the local shops for one-of-a-kind souvenirs, trendy fashion items, and Corsican specialties like honey, cheese, and olive oil.

Balagne Area

Balagne is famous for its attractive hilltop towns, olive orchards, vineyards, and magnificent seaside landscape. Here are some of the region's highlights:

- **Ile-Rousse**: Visit the lovely village of Ile-Rousse, noted for its sandy beaches, busy market square, and the town's name, red granite structures. Explore the vibrant streets, savor the local food, and unwind on the lovely Plage de l'Ostriconi.

- **Calenzana**: Depart from Calenzana, a gorgeous mountain town, on the famed GR20 hiking track. The walk provides stunning views of the surrounding landscapes, which include lush woods, steep peaks, and secret waterfalls.

- **Sant'Antonino**: Explore the hilltop town of Sant'Antonino, regarded as one of France's most beautiful villages. Wander through its small cobblestone alleyways, appreciate the flower-adorned antique stone buildings, and take in panoramic views of the surrounding countryside and sea.

Piana Calanques

The Calanques de Piana, a UNESCO World Heritage site, is a natural wonder located on the western coast of Corsica. This stunning stretch of coastline is characterized by its dramatic red granite cliffs, hidden coves, and crystal-clear waters. Here's what you can experience in the Calanques de Piana:

- **Scenic Drive**: Take a scenic drive along the D81 road, which winds through the Calanques de Piana. Marvel at the breathtaking rock formations, including the iconic Capo Rosso and the "Tête de Chien" (Dog's Head). Numerous viewpoints along the way offer unparalleled vistas of the cliffs and the Mediterranean Sea.

- **Boat excursion:** From Porto or Piana, take a boat excursion to see the Calanques up close. Cruise through tight passageways, explore isolated bays and marvel at the geological marvels of the towering cliffs from the sea. Keep a watch out for water life, such as dolphins and seagulls.

- **Hiking**: Put on your hiking boots and discover the Calanques de Piana's numerous pathways.

Follow the signs to find secret beaches, natural pools, and unusual rock formations. The routes vary in difficulty, guaranteeing that there is something for every hiking aficionado.

The breathtaking scenery, historical riches, and true Corsican charm of the Calvi and Balagne area, as well as the intriguing Calanques de Piana, entice visitors. Immerse yourself in the grandeur of this area, indulge in traditional cuisine, and make unforgettable memories in Corsica's heart.

Porto-Vecchio and the South Coast

The Porto-Vecchio area, located on Corsica's southeastern coast, combines gorgeous beaches, historical history, and natural treasures. Let's take a closer look at the highlights of this region:

City Guide to Porto-Vecchio

Porto-Vecchio is a thriving coastal town recognized for its lively atmosphere, lovely old town, and beautiful beaches. Here's a step-by-step guide to making the most of your visit:

- Old Town: Begin your journey in Porto-Vecchio's old town, where narrow cobblestone alleyways lead to lovely squares and ancient buildings. Discover the 16th-century Bastion de France, which provides panoramic views of the port and its environs. Visit the Church of St. Jean Baptiste, a magnificent structure with historic walls and a lovely interior.

- **Marina and Port**: Walk around the marina, which is dotted with yachts and sailing boats. Savor fresh seafood and regional delicacies at one of the waterfront eateries. The port area is also the starting point for boat trips to adjacent islands and hidden beaches.

- **Palombaggia and Santa Giulia Beaches**: Visit the well-known Palombaggia and Santa Giulia beaches, which are known for their immaculate white sand, crystal-clear seas, and scenic scenery. Spend your days sunbathing, swimming, and participating in water activities like snorkeling and paddleboarding. Don't miss out on the spectacular sunset views over the turquoise sea.

Bonifacio and Lavezzi Islands

Bonifacio, nestled above towering limestone cliffs on Corsica's southern coast, is a town steeped in history and spectacular in natural beauty. The adjacent Lavezzi Islands add to the area's attractiveness. Here's what you should know:

- **Bonifacio Citadel**: Begin your journey at the walled town of Bonifacio Citadel, which has tiny lanes, historic residences, and beautiful perspectives. Explore the historic citadel walls, pay a visit to the Church of St. Dominique, and take in panoramic views of the Bonifacio port and the Bonifacio Strait.

- **Bonifacio Old Town**: Stroll through the picturesque streets dotted with shops, cafés, and restaurants in Bonifacio's old town. Explore local artisan stores, dine on authentic Corsican cuisine, and take in the colorful ambiance of this old town.

- **Lavezzi Islands**: From Bonifacio, take a boat trip to the Lavezzi Islands, a tiny archipelago known for its beautiful beaches and crystal-clear seas. Explore deserted islands, go snorkeling to see beautiful marine life, and unwind on isolated stretches of beach.

Alta Rocca Area

The Alta Rocca area, situated inland from Porto-Vecchio, combines rough mountains, deep woods, and attractive settlements. Here are some of the highlights of this hilly area:

- **Zonza**: Explore the lovely town of Zonza, which is tucked among the mountain ranges. Explore the old stone buildings, stroll along the cobblestone streets, and take in panoramic views of the surrounding countryside.

- **Bavella Needles**: Take in the breathtaking Bavella Needles, a spectacular mountain range with towering granite peaks. Hike the well-marked paths, wonder at the spectacular views, and marvel at the unusual rock formations.

- **Aiguilles de Bavella**: Visit the Aiguilles de Bavella, a collection of granite spires with excellent rock climbing and canyoning options. Experience adrenaline-pumping activities in the middle of breathtaking natural beauty.

With its quaint town, gorgeous beaches, an old fortress, and magnificent natural scenery, the Porto-Vecchio area is a must-see.

encourages you to immerse yourself in its splendor and create lasting memories of your Corsican journey.

Corte and the Central Mountains

Corte, situated in the center of Corsica, is a scenic place with rocky mountains, green valleys, and a rich historical past. To make the most of your vacation, check out the following sites and activities:

Corte City Guide

Corte, Corsica's medieval capital, is a lovely town hidden among stunning natural surroundings. Here's a comprehensive introduction to the highlights of Corte:

- **Citadel of Corte**: Begin your trip with a visit to the Citadel of Corte, a medieval fortification with panoramic views of the town and its surrounds. Explore the region's history by walking through its old walls, towers, and courtyards.

- **Museu di a Corsica:** Visit the Museu di a Corsica, which is housed inside the Citadel, to learn more about Corsica's culture, customs, and history. The displays of the museum feature artifacts, archaeological discoveries, and artworks that represent the island's distinct past.

- **Place Paoli:** Take a walk around Place Paoli, Corte's principal plaza. It is a busy center where residents and tourists meet to relax, interact, and enjoy the lively environment. It is lined with attractive cafés, boutiques, and restaurants.

- **University of Corsica Pascal Paoli**: Discover the University of Corsica Pascal Paoli, which breathes new life into Corte. The campus has a contemporary architecture that mixes in wonderfully with the natural surroundings. Take a stroll around campus and take in the combination of education and nature.

Restonica Valley

The Restonica Valley, located near Corte, is a natural paradise with incomparable beauty and outdoor experiences. The following are the main sights and activities to enjoy in this enthralling valley:

- **Hiking routes**: Put on your hiking boots and go out on one of the Restonica Valley's numerous picturesque routes. The routes lead to breathtaking places like Lac de Melo and Lac de Capitello, two glacial lakes encircled by towering hills. Immerse yourself in the tranquil ambiance as you stroll through waterfalls, lush woods, and alpine meadows.

- **Swimming and Picnicking**: Take a relaxing plunge in the Restonica River's crystal-clear waters. There are wonderful picnic sites along its banks where you may rest, have a meal, and absorb the quiet of nature.

- **Mountaintop Views**: Visit Tavignano Gorges or Monte Rotondu for stunning panoramic views of the Restonica Valley. From these vantage points, you may take in the stunning sceneries, which includes rocky mountains, rich greenery, and a flowing river.

Castagniccia Region
The Castagniccia area, noted for its beautiful landscapes and cultural history, provides an insight into Corsica's traditional way of **life. Here are some of the attractions of this enthralling region:**

-**Village of Cervione**: Visit Cervione, a community known for its authenticity and breathtaking views of the surrounding countryside. Wander through its small lanes, observe the old stone buildings, and pay a visit to the architecturally significant Church of San Erasmo.

- **Chestnut Forests:** Marvel at the splendor of Castagniccia's chestnut woods. Take leisurely walks along the forest paths, take in the pure mountain air, and enjoy the peaceful atmosphere of these lush forests.

- **Cultural Heritage**: Immerse yourself in Castagniccia's cultural legacy by visiting the region's many chapels, cathedrals, and medieval convents. Corsican craftsmanship, religious items, and centuries-old customs are on display at these ancient locations.

- **Local Cuisine**: Savor traditional Corsican cuisine produced with local ingredients to immerse yourself in the region's tastes. Try the region's chestnut-based specialties, handmade cheeses, and fragrant wines.

Corte and the Central Mountains provide a one-of-a-kind combination of history, environment, and cultural diversity. Whether you're visiting Corte, trekking through the breathtaking Restonica Valley, or immersing yourself in the charm of the Castagniccia area, you're sure to make wonderful experiences in this enchanting corner of Corsica.

Must-Visit Destinations

Bonifacio

Bonifacio is a charming town on Corsica's southern point famed for its stunning cliffs, a medieval fortress, and adjacent archipelago. Discover the enchantments that make Bonifacio a must-see destination:

Citadel of Bonifacio

The Bonifacio Citadel towers above the town and the Mediterranean Sea. Explore the citadel's features, which include:

Bastion de l'Etendard: Begin your adventure in the citadel by seeing the Bastion de l'Etendard, a 13th-century stronghold. Take a guided tour to learn about the history, defense techniques, and architectural elements of the citadel.

Sainte-Marie-Majeure Church: Inside the citadel, see the Sainte-Marie-Majeure Church, a beautiful house of worship. Its exquisite Gothic architecture, antique paintings, and rich ornaments will astound you.

The Bonifacio Museum, housed inside the citadel, delves into the history and culture of Bonifacio. The museum displays archaeological items, marine exhibits, and artworks illustrating the town's history.

Take a leisurely stroll over the citadel walls and explore its defensive towers, such as Torra di Santa Maria and Torra di Sant'Agostino. Views of the town, the port, and the blue seas below are spectacular.

The Bonifacio Citadel is appropriate for families, however, small children may need monitoring owing to the high cliffs and restricted walkways.

Other sites: Because the citadel is in the center of Bonifacio, it is conveniently accessible to other sites like the King of Aragon's Staircase and boat cruises to the Lavezzi Islands.

Guided Tours: The citadel offers guided tours that provide important insights into its history, design, and defensive methods. A guided visit is needed to properly understand the citadel's importance.

King of Aragon's Staircase

The King of Aragon's Staircase is an architectural marvel and a tribute to Bonifacio's rich past. Here's what to anticipate from this famous landmark:

The King's Stairway, also known as the Escalier du Roi d'Aragon, is a natural stairway cut into the cliffs that leads down to the sea. It is said to have been cut in the 13th century by the Genoese and utilized as an escape route during times of strife.

Stairs & Walkways: Descend the staircase's steep stairs and meandering walkways, which have been meticulously cut into the cliffside. As you descend, take in the stunning rock formations, old caverns, and secret coves that dot the shoreline.

Scenic Boat Tours: Take a boat excursion at the bottom of the stairway to see the rough beauty of the coastline. Sail along the cliffs, marvel at the beautiful white limestone structures, and take in the gorgeous sea vistas of Bonifacio.

Due to the high stairs and rocky terrain, the King of Aragon's Staircase may not be suited for small children or persons with mobility concerns.

Proximity to Other sights: Because the staircase is close to the Bonifacio Citadel, travelers may easily combine their visits to both sights.

Guided Tours: There are no guided tours required to visit the King of Aragon's Staircase. To properly enjoy the coastline splendor and panoramic vistas, however, it is advised that you take a boat cruise at the bottom of the stairway.

Lavezzi Islands

The Lavezzi Islands, a beautiful archipelago famed for its natural beauty and abundant marine life, are just a short boat trip from Bonifacio. Here are some of the things you can do in this gorgeous island group:

Dive into the crystal-clear waters that surround the Lavezzi Islands to find an underwater paradise. Snorkel or scuba dive amid vibrant coral reefs, swim among schools of fish and come face to face with rare marine creatures.

White Sandy Beaches: Unwind on the Lavezzi Islands' exquisite white sandy beaches. In this pristine and serene setting, enjoy sunbathing, beachcombing, and picnics.

Hiking & Nature paths: Explore the islands on foot by following nature paths that take you through mountainous terrain with panoramic views of the Mediterranean Sea. Keep a look out for the various flora and creatures that call these islands home.

Family-Friendly: The Lavezzi Islands are an excellent family getaway, with chances for snorkeling, beachcombing, and exploring nature paths. Young children, on the other hand, should be monitored near the water.

Other Attractions: The Lavezzi Islands are just a short boat ride away from Bonifacio, making them ideal for a day excursion. Visits to the Bonifacio Citadel and the King of Aragon's Staircase are often combined.

Guided trips: For a more educational and structured experience, guided boat trips to the Lavezzi Islands are available and recommended. These trips often incorporate snorkeling and provide information about the marine life and history of the islands.

The Lavezzi Islands and Bonifacio provide a compelling combination of history, natural beauty, and coastal charm. You'll be fascinated by the unique experiences and stunning vistas found in this part of Corsica, whether you're touring the old citadel, climbing the King of Aragon's Staircase, or going to the pristine Lavezzi Islands.

Porto

Porto is a lovely beach community on Corsica's western coast recognized for its amazing natural beauty and accessibility to great attractions. Discover the features that make Porto a must-see destination:

Piana's Calanques

The Calanques de Piana are a series of breathtaking red granite cliffs and rock formations along the coast near Porto. Here's what you may find in this one-of-a-kind natural wonder:

picturesque Drive: Take a picturesque drive along the winding coastal road to see the Calanques de Piana from above. Admire the spectacular red cliffs, fascinating rock formations, and the contrast between the blue water and the bright landscape.

Hiking paths: Put on your hiking boots and go out to explore the trekking paths that wind through the Calanques de

Piana. Enjoy the breathtaking views as you travel across this rocky landscape in search of secret coves and beautiful beaches.

Sunset Views: Witness the sunset over the Calanques de Piana for wonderful memories. The setting sun's warm colors create a lovely environment, throwing an alluring light on the cliffs and producing an unforgettable experience.

Girolata Village

Girolata, located inside the Scandola Nature Reserve, is a lovely hamlet that can only be reached by boat or on foot. Here are some of the things you may do in this isolated and beautiful location:

Discover the tranquillity and solitude of Girolata, a community unaffected by contemporary development. Stroll through its small lanes, appreciate the historic stone buildings, and relax in its tranquil setting.

Hiking Opportunities: Take a picturesque trek from Porto to Girolata or via the neighboring hills. Immerse yourself in unspoiled nature while taking in magnificent views of the shoreline.

Beaches and Watersports: Spend time relaxing on the magnificent beaches around Girolata or participating in watersports activities like kayaking or paddleboarding. In this gorgeous beachfront location, enjoy the pristine waters and stunning surroundings.

The Scandola Nature Reserve, the intriguing Calanques de Piana, and the distant settlement of Girolata are just a few of Porto's natural beauties. Porto delivers a memorable experience in the midst of Corsica's natural splendor, whether exploring the reserve by boat, taking in the breathtaking views from the coastal road, or immersing yourself in the calm of Girolata.

Scandola National Park

The Scandola Nature Reserve is a beautiful natural beauty on Corsica's western coast. This UNESCO World Heritage Site provides a once-in-a-lifetime opportunity to witness Corsica's pristine beauty and complex environment. The following are the main facts regarding the Scandola Nature Reserve:

World Heritage Site (UNESCO)

The Scandola Nature Reserve was designated a UNESCO World Heritage Site in 1983 for its exceptional natural value and unique biological importance. The reserve is around 900 hectares in size and includes both land and marine ecosystems. It is a protected area dedicated to preserving the region's remarkable beauty and wildlife.

The reserve is known for its stunning scenery, which includes towering cliffs, quiet beaches, and secret coves. Its unusual red rock formations, carved by weathering over millions of years, provide a captivating and surreal landscape. The reserve's rich flora and animals contribute to its ecological significance.

Boat Tours & Activities

The greatest way to really appreciate the Scandola Nature Reserve's grandeur and immerse yourself in its natural delights is to explore it by boat. Several tour companies provide guided boat cruises, which provide guests with an educational and pleasant experience. Here's what to expect:

- **Lovely Cruises**: Take a lovely cruise along the Scandola Nature Reserve's shoreline. You'll be treated to breathtaking vistas of the majestic cliffs, secret caverns, and pristine beaches as you cruise across the blue seas. The educated guides on board will give comments on the area's geological formations, fauna, and conservation activities.

- **Wildlife Observation**: The reserve is home to a wide variety of marine and avian species. As you sail through the reserve, keep a look out for dolphins, seals, and seagulls. The pristine waters also provide good visibility for snorkeling and scuba diving, enabling you to explore the undersea world, which is teaming with colorful fish, coral reefs, and other marine life.

- **Geological Wonders**: The Scandola Nature Reserve's spectacular red rock formations and fascinating caverns are a photographer's delight. Capture nature's splendor as you go through small valleys and under towering cliffs. The wonderful mood is created by the play of light and shadow on the craggy terrain.

- **Nature Interpretation**: During boat trips, instructors share information about the reserve's geology, history, and ecological importance. Learn about the cliffs' creation, the effects of human activity on the region, and the continuing conservation efforts to maintain this unique habitat.

- **Entrance and Regulations**: Because the Scandola Nature Reserve is protected, entrance to specific places may be prohibited. To maintain the preservation of the reserve's sensitive ecology, it is essential to follow the restrictions and standards established by the reserve administration. Respect for animals, marine life, and the natural environment is essential.

The Scandola Nature Reserve is a once-in-a-lifetime opportunity to observe the raw beauty of Corsica's western coast. The reserve provides an extraordinary excursion into nature's magnificence, whether you're admiring the towering cliffs, observing animals, or sailing through secret tunnels.

Porto is a lovely beach community on Corsica's western coast recognized for its amazing natural beauty and accessibility to great attractions. Everything you need to know about Porto is right here:

- **Family-Friendly**: Porto is a family-friendly location that offers outdoor excursions and discovery for people of all ages. Children may enjoy boat trips, short treks, and beach activities, making it a great family holiday location.

- **Convenience to Other Attractions**: Porto is ideally positioned among other notable Corsican attractions. The Scandola Nature Reserve and the Calanques de Piana are also nearby, enabling tourists to see many sights in one day.

- **Guided excursions:** Guided excursions of the Scandola Nature Reserve and the Calanques de Piana are provided. These tours give interesting commentary and guarantee that guests get the most of their vacation by seeing the sights with expert guides.

- **Location**: Porto is located on Corsica's western coast, overlooking the Gulf of Porto. It is about a two-hour journey from Ajaccio and a three-hour trip from Bastia, making it readily accessible by car.

- **Scandola Nature Reserve**: The Scandola Nature Reserve, situated near Porto, provides stunning vistas, boat trips, and snorkeling and diving possibilities. It is a protected region recognized for its diverse marine life and breathtaking granite formations.

- **Calanques de Piana**: The Calanques de Piana are a group of dramatic red granite cliffs and rock formations near Porto. Visitors may take picturesque drives, wander along the paths, and watch the sunset over the cliffs.

- **Girolata town**: Girolata is a lonely seaside town accessible only by boat or on foot, tucked inside the Scandola Nature Reserve. It has a relaxing environment, hiking options, and excellent beaches for watersports.

- **Accommodation and Facilities**: Porto offers a variety of lodging alternatives, including hotels, guesthouses, and campgrounds. There are also restaurants, cafés, and stores to meet the requirements of guests.

Porto's closeness to natural sites, availability of guided excursions, family-friendly attitude, and breathtaking surroundings make it an ideal location for both families and people looking for a memorable Corsica experience.

Aiguilles de Bavella

The Aiguilles de Bavella are a beautiful mountain range in southern Corsica. This natural marvel draws outdoor enthusiasts from all over the globe because of its towering rock formations, rough terrain, and superb trekking options. Here's all you need to know about Aiguilles de Bavella:

Hiking Trails and Rock Formations

The Aiguilles de Bavella are famous for their spectacular rock formations that seem like needles piercing the sky. The region is a hiker's paradise, with a variety of paths for hikers of all ability levels. Here are some important notes regarding trekking in Bavella:

- **Hiking routes**: There are several hiking routes to select from, ranging from short strolls to difficult excursions. The GR20, a long-distance path that spans the island and travels through the Aiguilles de Bavella, is the most well-known trail. Because of its difficulty level and harsh terrain, this path is best suited for experienced hikers. There are various day paths accessible for individuals looking for shorter walks, such as the Trou de la Bombe and the Plateau du Cuscione.

- **Scenic Beauty:** Bavella's hiking routes provide beautiful views of the surrounding mountains, woods, and rock formations. As you walk the routes, take in the rocky peaks, deep gorges, and panoramic panoramas. The landscape's hues and textures form a breathtaking visual spectacle, offering numerous chances for photography and immersing yourself in nature's magnificence.

- **Natural Pools and Waterfalls**: Natural pools and waterfalls may be found along several of the hiking paths, providing delightful locations to cool down and rest. Take a plunge in the crystal-clear waters or enjoy a picnic in the midst of nature's tranquility.

- **Flora and Fauna**: The Aiguilles de Bavella are home to a wide variety of plant and animal life. Hiking along the paths will expose you to rich greenery such as Corsican pines, wildflowers, and scented plants. Keep a watch out for animals including wild boars, deer, and other bird species.

Bavella Adventure Activities

Aside from trekking, the Aiguilles de Bavella area has a variety of exhilarating adventure activities for adrenaline junkies. Here are some adventurous activities you may partake in:

- **Rock Climbing**: Bavella's towering granite formations create a great playground for rock climbers. The craggy cliffs provide a variety of routes and degrees of difficulty for both novice and expert climbers. While surrounded by breathtaking mountain vistas, put your talents to the test and tackle the sheer heights.

- **Canyoning:** Canyoning tours allow you to explore the natural canyons and gorges of Bavella. Descend down falling waterfalls, explore small passageways, and bathe in cool pools. Canyoning trips are offered for all ability levels and provide a unique view of the rough landscape.

- **Via Ferrata**: Try via ferrata in Bavella for an exciting experience that mixes hiking and rock climbing. This sport entails crossing a safe mountain path outfitted with ropes, ladders, and iron rungs. It provides a safe but thrilling way to enjoy the Aiguilles de Bavella's raw splendor.

- **Mountain biking**: Bavella's tough terrain and picturesque scenery make it an ideal location for mountain riding. Rent a bike or go on a guided tour to explore the trails and experience the adrenaline rush of downhill rides in the middle of stunning mountain panoramas.

The Aiguilles de Bavella is rather simple to reach, with a well-maintained road connecting to the mountain range's core. Parking spots are also provided for individuals who choose to drive to the trailheads. Before beginning on hiking other adventure activities in Bavella, it's a good idea to check the weather, route difficulties, and any permits or laws.

The Aiguilles de Bavella provide an intriguing blend of natural beauty, tough paths, and exhilarating adventure sports. Whether trekking through the steep peaks, ascending the rock formations, or bicycling across the hilly environment, Bavella provides an exceptional outdoor adventure in Corsica's core.

L'Île-Rousse

L'Île-Rousse is a lovely coastal village on Corsica's northwest coast. L'Île-Rousse is a popular destination for both residents and visitors due to its clean beaches, old buildings, and laid-back environment. Let's get into the specifics of what makes L'Île-Rousse a must-see destination:

Town and Beaches

L'Île-Rousse has a charming town center with a lively ambiance and a variety of activities. What to anticipate while visiting the town and its stunning beaches:

- **Town Center**: Take a stroll around L'Île-Rousse's town center and breathe in the distinctive atmosphere. Admire the pastel-colored houses, small lanes, and lively squares of typical Mediterranean architecture. Explore the local stores, boutiques, and markets for a wide range of things such as handicrafts, fresh fruit, and souvenirs.

- **Place Paoli**: L'Île-Rousse's main plaza, Place Paoli, is a hive of activity. Sip a coffee or a refreshing beverage at one of the outdoor cafés while watching the world go by. The plaza also holds frequent markets and festivals, which contribute to the area's bustling and colorful ambiance.

- **L'Île-Rousse Market**: Don't miss out on the L'Île-Rousse market, which is held every day in Place Paoli. Explore vendors offering fresh fruits and vegetables, cheeses, cured meats, and regional delicacies. Immerse yourself in Corsican cuisine's bright colors, smells, and tastes.

- **Beaches**: L'Île-Rousse is well-known for its beautiful beaches, which have brilliant blue seas and smooth golden sand. The Plage de l'Île-Rousse is conveniently placed in the heart of the city. Sunbathe, swim, and relax on the beach, or participate in water activities such as paddleboarding, kayaking, and jet skiing. For a more tranquil experience, visit adjacent beaches such as Plage de Bodri and Plage de Lozari.

Pietra Lighthouse

The Pietra Lighthouse, perched on a rocky outcrop overlooking the sea, is a significant landmark in L'Île-Rousse. This historic site has the following attractions:

- **Historical Importance**: The Pietra Lighthouse, also known as the Phare de la Pietra, was built in the late 1800s. It was a significant navigational aid for ships approaching L'Île-

Rousse's harbor. It now serves as a reminder of the town's maritime history.

- **Scenic Views**: Ascend to the Pietra Lighthouse for panoramic views of the town, the surrounding coastline, and the glistening Mediterranean Sea. The lofty vantage point provides stunning perspectives ideal for photography or just admiring the natural beauty of the region.

- **Sunset Spot**: The Pietra Lighthouse is well-known for its spectacular sunset views. As the sun sets, the sky changes into a rainbow of hues, creating a magnificent light over the town and the sea. The sunset from the lighthouse is an unforgettable event that should not be missed.

L'Île-Rousse and its renowned Pietra Lighthouse provide a unique combination of natural beauty, historical charm, and seaside tranquility. L'Île-Rousse guarantees a lovely and unique experience on the Corsican coast, whether you're visiting the busy town center, lazing on the beautiful beaches, or appreciating the panoramic views from the lighthouse.

Outdoor Activities

Routes for Hiking and Trekking

Corsica has a vast network of hiking and trekking paths that appeal to all ability levels and provide breathtaking views of the island's various landscapes. Here are three noteworthy routes:

The GR20 Trail

The GR20 is a famed long-distance path that runs from north to south over Corsica's hilly terrain, covering around 180 kilometers (112 miles). Here is some further information regarding this famous trail:

- **Difficulty Level**: The GR20 is regarded as one of Europe's most difficult paths, requiring exceptional physical condition and trekking expertise. It has steep ascents and descents, difficult trails, and exposed areas that need careful planning and endurance.

- **Scenic Highlights**: The GR20 takes hikers through magnificent landscapes, including granite peaks, lush forests, glacial lakes, and alpine meadows. Along the route, you'll see breathtaking views, gorgeous valleys, and rare flora and animals.

- **Refuges and Campsites**: Hikers may rest, find shelter, and refill supplies in mountain refuges along the way. These shelters provide basic necessities such as mattresses, bathing, and food. For those who like to camp, there are additional campsites available.

- **Time**: Completing the GR20 normally takes 15 to 16 days, however, this might vary depending on your speed and schedule. If you prefer shorter treks, you may also tackle shorter parts of the path.

Mare e Monti

The Mare e Monti Trail blends coastal and alpine terrain, providing a varied and intriguing trekking experience. More information about this path may be found here:

- **Scenic Diversity**: Hikers may enjoy Corsica's coastline beauties as well as its inner mountain areas on the Mare e Monti Trail. Beautiful views of the blue sea, sandy beaches, towering cliffs, deep woods, lovely towns, and rolling hills await you.

- **Difficulty Level**: The Mare e Monti Trail is somewhat demanding, making it appropriate for hikers with average fitness and some hiking experience. It has some steep portions but is typically less difficult than the GR20.

- **Duration**: The full Mare e Monti Trail typically takes 10 to 12 days to complete, however, this may be changed depending on your tastes and available time. You may also choose shorter portions of the path or day treks.

- **Accommodation**: The Mare e Monti Trail offers a variety of lodging alternatives, including campgrounds, guesthouses, and mountain refuges. These give nice rest stops as well as the opportunity to appreciate the hospitality of the locals.

Monte Cinto Summit

Conquering the peak of Monte Cinto is an exceptional expedition for experienced hikers and mountaineers looking for a thrilling challenge. Here's everything you need to know:

- **Corsica's Highest Peak**: Monte Cinto is the highest point in Corsica, reaching an amazing height of 2,706 meters (8,878 feet). Technical abilities, climbing equipment, and awareness of alpine ecosystems are required to reach the peak.

- **Alpine Setting**: The climb to Monte Cinto takes you through an alpine setting with steep ridges, difficult terrain, and the odd snowfield. When you reach the peak, you'll be rewarded with breathtaking views of Corsica's mountains and coastline.

- **Guided Tours**: Due to the challenging nature of the climb, joining a guided tour conducted by experienced mountain guides is highly suggested. They can supply the essential equipment and knowledge, as well as assure the ascent's safety.

- **Weather Considerations**: Because the weather in the mountains may change quickly, it's important to check the forecast and plan your trek appropriately. Always prioritize safety and be prepared for weather and visibility changes.

Corsica's hiking and trekking paths provide outdoor lovers with a variety of possibilities. Corsica has a plethora of natural beauty and adventure for hikers and nature lovers, whether you're ready for the challenge of the GR20, the different vistas of the Mare e Monti Trail, or the exciting trek to Monte Cinto's top. While exploring these routes, remember to prepare sufficiently, obey safety requirements, and respect the environment.

Beaches and Water Sports

Corsica is known for its scenic beaches and crystal-clear seas, which provide a wide range of water sports for people of all ages and interests. Corsica has a plethora of beautiful beaches, each with its own distinct traits. Here are some of the best beaches to visit:

- **Palombaggia Beach**: Palombaggia Beach, located near Porto-Vecchio in the south, is a postcard-perfect beach noted for its pristine white beaches, blue seas, and thick pine forest background. It has beach bars, restaurants, and rentals for water sports equipment.

- **Santa Giulia Beach**

A lovely crescent-shaped bay with shallow, crystal-clear seas and smooth golden beaches, Santa Giulia Beach is another popular alternative near Porto-Vecchio. The beach is great for families with children and provides water sports such as paddleboarding and jet skiing.

- Rondinara Beach

Rondinara Beach, located between Porto-Vecchio and Bonifacio, is widely recognized as one of Corsica's most beautiful beaches. Its horseshoe shape provides a secluded cove with calm seas, ideal for swimming, snorkeling, and sunbathing. The neighboring hills provide for a beautiful background.

- Saleccia Beach

Located in northern Corsica's Agriates Desert, Saleccia Beach provides a lonely and unspoilt location. This gorgeous beach, accessible by boat or a difficult trek, has turquoise seas, fine white beaches, and a quiet ambiance. It's a great place for sunbathing and picnics.

- Calanques de Piana Beaches

The Calanques de Piana provide spectacular scenery with towering red granite cliffs plummeting into the water along the western coast near Porto. While the beaches in this region aren't very large, they do provide isolated coves and crystal-clear seas for swimming and snorkeling.

Snorkeling and Diving Spot

The pristine seas of Corsica make it an ideal location for snorkeling and diving aficionados. Here are a few prominent locations

- Scandola Nature Reserve

A UNESCO World Heritage Site, the Scandola Nature Reserve is a biodiversity-rich maritime wonderland. Divers and snorkelers may explore the reserve's protected waters, where they can find colorful fish, brilliant coral reefs, and underwater caverns.

- Lavezzi Islands

The Lavezzi Islands are a natural marine reserve off the southern edge of Corsica near Bonifacio. The islands provide excellent snorkeling and diving possibilities, with crystal-clear seas and a plethora of marine life. Swimming amid schools of fish, exploring rocky formations, and marveling at the colourful underwater environment are all options.

- Revellata Peninsula

The Revellata Peninsula, located near Calvi, is a famous diving site. Its rocky shoreline is riddled with caves, arches, and marine canyons, making for an interesting underwater scene to explore. Divers may see octopuses, groupers, and colorful sponges among other marine animals.

Water sports and boat rentals

Corsica's coastal regions are perfect for a variety of water sports and activities. Here are some common alternatives:

- Kayaking and Stand-Up Paddleboarding

Rent a kayak or stand-up paddleboard to explore Corsica's coastline at your own speed. Glide over the tranquil waters, find secret coves, and take in the scenery of the surrounding countryside. Many seaside communities provide rental services.

- Jet Skiing and Parasailing

Jet skiing and parasailing are thrilling adventures for adrenaline seekers. Rent a jet ski and ride the waves, or try parasailing for a bird's-eye view of the shore. Popular beach locations like as Porto-Vecchio, Ajaccio, and Calvi provide these sports.

- Boat Rentals and Excursions

Renting a boat is an excellent way to explore the coastline and adjacent islands of Corsica. Select from a modest motorboat to a large yacht and go on your own trip. Alternatively, you may go on a guided boat tour to see secret beaches, sea caves, and other gorgeous sites.

The beaches and water activities of Corsica provide many chances for leisure, adventure, and discovery. Corsica offers something for everyone, whether you like relaxing on lovely beaches, snorkeling in clean seas, or participating in exhilarating water sports.

Rock Climbing and Canyoning

The varied geography of Corsica provides interesting options for rock climbing and canyoning aficionados. Here are the specifics of these adrenaline-pumping sports, which range from steep mountains to deep gorges:

Popular Climbing Locations

Corsica is a rock climber's paradise, with various climbing areas appropriate for all levels of expertise. Here are a few popular climbing spots:

- The Aiguilles de Bavella in the Bavella Massif is a well-known rock climbing location. It has magnificent granite spires and cliffs with a variety of climbing routes ranging from beginner to difficult. The paths provide spectacular views of the surrounding mountains and woods.

- Restonica Valley: The Restonica Valley, located near Corte, has good climbing possibilities. The valley has spectacular granite cliffs and routes for both conventional and sport climbers. Climbers may take in the splendor of the valley while facing a variety of difficult ascents.

- Calanques de Piana: The Calanques de Piana, near Porto, provide not only beautiful coastline views but also a unique climbing experience. The towering red granite cliffs along the beach provide demanding routes as well as a spectacular view of the Mediterranean Sea.

- Tavignano Gorge: Located near Corte, the Tavignano Gorge is a famous destination for adventure climbers. The gorge is characterized by towering limestone cliffs and trails of various difficulty. Climbers may take in the natural splendor of the valley while tackling the difficult ascents.

- Capo Rosso: Capo Rosso, near Piana, provides beautiful seaside climbing chances. Climbers will find the red granite cliffs overlooking the sea to be both stunning and demanding. The routes vary in complexity, making them appropriate for both novice and expert climbers.

Canyoning in the Corsican Gorges
Corsica's gorges provide the perfect playground for canyoning enthusiasts, combining hiking, swimming, and rappelling through stunning natural landscapes. Here are some notable canyoning spots

- **Verghellu Gorge**: Located in the Restonica Valley near Corte, the Verghellu Gorge is a famous canyoning site in Corsica. The gorge provides an exciting canyoning experience, with dives into deep pools, natural water slides, and waterfall rappelling.

- **Richiusa Gorge**: The Richiusa Gorge, located in the Prunelli Valley, is noted for its scenic splendor and adventurous canyoning courses. The canyon's waterfalls, pools, and tiny sections provide an exciting and adventurous canyoning experience.

- **Pulischellu Gorge**: The Pulischellu Gorge, located near Bavella, provides a canyoning trip surrounded by stunning scenery. There are rappels, jumps, and natural slides in the canyon, as well as blue pools etched into the rock formations.

- **Zoicu Gorge**: The Zoicu Gorge, located in the Asco Valley, is noted for its crystal-clear streams and difficult canyoning courses. The canyon provides a fantastic canyoning experience for adrenaline junkies by combining rappelling, jumps, and swimming through tiny sections.

- **Fium'Orbo Gorge**: Located near Ghisonaccia, the Fium'Orbo Gorge is a canyoning hidden treasure. The gorge is filled with flowing waterfalls, natural slides, and deep pools, making for an amazing canyoning trip in a beautiful location.

It is critical to prioritize safety and assess the competence necessary for each area while participating in rock climbing and canyoning activities. To guarantee a safe and pleasurable trip, it is advised that you travel with professional guides or join scheduled excursions.

Boating and sailing

Corsica's gorgeous coastline, pristine seas, and several marinas provide a multitude of choices for sailing and boating lovers. Whether you're an expert sailor or a novice seeking for a relaxing voyage, below are the specifics on sailing and boating activities in Corsica

Sailing Routes and Yacht Charters

- **boat Charters**: There are various firms in Corsica that specialize in boat charters. They provide a variety of alternatives, such as sailboats, catamarans, and luxury yachts, enabling you to choose the vessel that best meets your interests and party size. You may charter a boat for a day, a week, or longer, allowing you to explore the coastline of Corsica at your own speed.

- **Sailing Routes**: Corsica has a plethora of picturesque sailing routes that highlight the island's natural beauty. Popular itineraries include sailing from Ajaccio to Calvi on the west coast, exploring the east coast from Bastia to Bonifacio, and circumnavigating the whole island. These paths provide a range of scenery, such as stunning cliffs, hidden coves, and lovely beaches. They also allow you to stop in at attractive seaside towns and villages along the route.

- **Moorings and Marinas**: There are a variety of marinas and mooring locations around the Corsican coast where you may berth your yacht or boat. Ajaccio, Calvi, Bonifacio, and Porto-Vecchio are among the major marinas. Fuel stations, restaurants, bathroom facilities, and resupply choices are all available at these marinas. It's best to make reservations ahead of time, particularly during high tourist season.

- **Navigation and Weather**: It is important to be conversant with navigation laws and local maritime regulations before setting sail in Corsica. The seas of the island may be exposed to high winds, particularly in the Strait of Bonifacio, so pay attention to weather predictions and plan your sailing schedule appropriately. Furthermore, nautical charts and GPS navigation equipment are available to aid navigation and provide a safe and comfortable sailing trip.

Day Trips and Coastal Cruises

- **coastline Cruises**: If you want a more laid-back boating experience, coastline cruises are a great choice. Several tour companies provide coastal cruises that enable you to explore Corsica's gorgeous coastline while discovering hidden jewels along the route. These excursions often feature stops at gorgeous beaches, quiet coves, and stunning overlooks, allowing you to swim, snorkel, and take in the spectacular scenery. Sun decks, lounges, and eating places are among the onboard facilities that assure your comfort during the voyage.

- **Day excursions**: Day excursions are a popular option for a shorter sailing experience. These excursions usually leave coastal towns and take you on a picturesque journey to local sights. To observe the abundant marine life under the surface, you may visit picturesque beaches, explore sea caves, and participate in guided snorkeling lessons. Individuals, couples, and families may enjoy day tours that showcase Corsica's seaside splendor.

- **picturesque Routes**: Many boating trips in Corsica take you through picturesque routes where you may see renowned sites and natural treasures. You may, for example, travel along the coast at Porto-Vecchio, admiring the white limestone cliffs and secret bays. Alternatively, you may visit the Calanques de Piana, where towering red granite cliffs meet the turquoise Mediterranean waves. These pathways provide fantastic picture possibilities as well as breathtaking vistas of Corsica's coastal scenery.

- **Fishing Trips**: Fishing enthusiasts can indulge in fishing charters or guided fishing trips in Corsica's abundant fishing grounds. These trips cater to both beginners and experienced anglers, providing the necessary equipment and local expertise to enhance your fishing experience. Whether you're interested in deep-sea fishing or prefer a more leisurely experience, there are options available to suit your preferences.

When sailing or boating, it is essential to emphasize safety and adhere to maritime regulations. If you have no sailing expertise, consider hiring a skipper to manage navigation and guarantee a safe cruise. Always check the weather and sea predictions before setting off, and have the required safety equipment aboard. Finally, practice responsible boating, which includes appropriate trash disposal and preventing harm to coral reefs and other fragile ecosystems.

Wildlife Watching

Corsica's various ecosystems and beautiful natural landscapes make it an ideal vacation for nature lovers. Here are the information of wildlife observing activities in Corsica, ranging from birding to interactions with marine life:

Birdwatching Locations

- **Bonifatu Forest**: Located in the Balagne area, Bonifatu Forest is a birdwatcher's paradise. Several bird species live in the woodland, including the Corsican nuthatch, Bonelli's eagle, and Eurasian eagle-owl. Explore the woodland pathways while keeping an eye out for these amazing bird species.

- **Étang de Biguglia**: This vast lagoon and natural reserve near Bastia draws a broad range of bird species. This region is rich in birdlife, with everything from flamingos and herons to warblers and waders. Visitors may immerse themselves in the reserve's diverse birdlife by visiting observation spots and walking pathways.

- **L'Étang de Diana**: L'Étang de Diana, located near Aléria, is another major wetland habitat for birding in Corsica. It is a Natura 2000 site and home to a variety of bird species, including the greater flamingo, black-winged stilt, and tiny tern. Take a trip along the observation trails to see and photograph these magnificent birds.

- **Cap Corse**: The craggy peninsula of Cap Corse provides excellent birding possibilities, especially during migratory seasons. Along the coastal cliffs and in the maritime regions, look for raptors like the short-toed snake eagle and the red kite, as well as seabirds like the European shag and the Audouin's gull.

Marine Life and Dolphin Watching
- **Strait of Bonifacio**: The Strait of Bonifacio, which connects Corsica and Sardinia, is known for its diverse marine species. It is home to a variety of dolphin species, including the common and bottlenose dolphins. To see these wonderful

animals in their natural environment, take a guided boat trip or a dolphin-watching excursion. Remember that good dolphin viewing entails keeping a safe distance and respecting their behavior.

- **Scandola Nature Reserve:** A UNESCO World Heritage Site, the Scandola Nature Reserve is noted not just for its breathtaking vistas but also for its flourishing marine life. Various fish, sea turtles, and marine animals call the reserve home. Take a boat tour or go snorkeling in the reserve's protected waters to see the diverse marine life and perhaps glimpse dolphins, seals, and other aquatic critters.

- **Lavezzi Islands**: The Lavezzi Islands, situated near Bonifacio, provide excellent prospects for interactions with aquatic life. The island's crystal-clear waters are rich with marine species, including colorful fish, octopuses, and sea urchins. Explore the undersea world and get up close and personal with the amazing marine life by snorkeling or diving in these clean waters.

It is important to respect the animals and their habitats while partaking in wildlife viewing activities. Maintain a safe distance from animals and follow any rules offered by tour companies or nature reserves. When birding, use binoculars or a telephoto lens to see the birds without disturbing them. Furthermore, follow safe snorkeling and diving techniques such as avoiding harming or disturbing marine creatures and being sensitive to the delicate underwater ecosystem.

101

102

CHAPTER FOUR
Corsican Dining and Cuisine

Corsican cuisine is known for its rich tastes, fresh ingredients, and culinary influences from Italy and France. Immerse yourself in the culinary pleasures of Corsica with the traditional meals and sweets listed below:

Corsican charcuterie

The charcuterie of Corsica is a great hallmark of the island's gastronomic tradition. It offers a variety of cured meats and sausages, each with a particular taste. Here are a few noteworthy examples:

- **Lonzu**: A dry-cured pork filet marinated in wine, garlic, and herbs before hanging to dry. It has a delicate taste with a tinge of sweetness and is often eaten thinly sliced. The marination process infuses aromatic compounds into the meat, resulting in a distinct flavor.

Coppa: Coppa is produced from the pig's neck muscle and is seasoned with herbs and spices. It is air-dried to produce soft and tasty cured meat. Coppa has a somewhat salty and savory flavor, with undertones of pepper and herbs that enhance the pork's, inherent sweetness.

- **Figatellu**: A Corsican sausage prepared from pig liver, pancetta, and spices, Figatellu is a one-of-a-kind product. It is often grilled or pan-fried and has a rich and delicious flavor. The mix of hog liver, pancetta, and spices results in a tasty and somewhat gamey sausage that is popular among both residents and tourists.

- **Prisuttu**: Prisuttu is the Corsican equivalent of prosciutto. It's a dry-cured ham prepared from the pig's rear leg, seasoned with local herbs, and kept for months to acquire its characteristic taste. The flavor of Prisuttu is delicate and somewhat salty, with a melt-in-your-mouth texture. It is often served thinly sliced with local cheeses and bread.

Fiadone and Other Desserts

Corsican cuisine also includes wonderful sweets that are a must-try when visiting. Here are a few examples of traditional sweet treats:

- **Fiadone**: Fiadone is a Corsican cheesecake prepared with brocciu, an island-exclusive fresh cheese. It is often flavored with lemon zest and, sometimes, orange blossom water. The creamy brocciu cheese and citrus tastes combine to make a light and delicious treat. Fiadone is often cooked until a golden crust develops on top, lending a lovely texture to the creamy inside.

Canistrelli: Canistrelli are typical Corsican biscuits available in a variety of flavors such as anise, lemon, and almond. These cookies have a crumbly texture and a sweet flavor. They are often served with coffee or as a sweet snack. Canistrelli are ideal for dipping into coffee or tea to enable the flavors to combine for a delectable treat.

- **Fiadone au Brocciu**: This baked delicacy is created with brocciu cheese, eggs, sugar, and lemon zest. It has a delicate taste and a custard-like consistency. The brocciu cheese adds a particular acidic flavor to the dish, while the eggs and sugar form a creamy and sweet basis. The addition of lemon zest gives the dish a delightful citrus scent.

- Chestnut-based sweets: Corsica is noted for its abundance of chestnut trees, which are prominently featured in numerous sweets. There is a range of chestnut-based delights to satiate your sweet craving, ranging from chestnut flour crepes to chestnut mousse and chestnut cake. Chestnut flour gives the pastries a rich and earthy flavor that is strongly established in Corsican culinary traditions.

Explore the local cuisine and seek traditional delicacies while eating in Corsica. Many restaurants and cafes provide Corsican delicacies, enabling you to experience the island's genuine tastes. To improve the gastronomic experience, pair your meals with local wines such as Nielluccio or Vermentino. For a thorough gourmet voyage across the island's culinary traditions, don't forget to indulge in Corsica's famed olive oil, honey, and handmade cheeses such as brocciu or tomme.

Popular Local Restaurants

Dining in local restaurants is a fantastic opportunity to enjoy the unique tastes and culinary traditions of the island while exploring Corsican cuisine. Here are some popular restaurant choices in Corsica's major cities:

Restaurant Recommendations in Ajaccio

- Le 20123 Restaurant: Located in the center of Ajaccio, Le 20123 provides a great dining experience with an emphasis on local Corsican delicacies. Traditional meals with a contemporary touch are included on the menu, which features fresh seafood, charcuterie, and seasonal veggies. The main meals vary in price from €20 to €35.

- **A Casa Corsa**: A Casa Corsa, located in Ajaccio's ancient town, is noted for its friendly and welcoming environment. The restaurant serves Corsican cuisine, including wild boar stew, grilled meats, and handmade cheeses. The main meals vary in price from €15 to €30.

- **Chez Seraphin**: This Ajaccio family-run restaurant has a nice environment and cuisine including traditional Corsican delicacies. Chez Seraphin provides something for everyone, from Corsican charcuterie plates to seafood risotto and delicious stews. The main meals vary in price from €15 to €30.

Restaurant Recommendations in Bastia

- **U Fanale**: U Fanale is a well-known restaurant in the centre of Bastia. It has a comfortable and pleasant ambience, as well as a cuisine that focuses on Corsican delicacies. For a fantastic dining experience, try their wild boar ragout, seafood spaghetti, or their famed Fiadone cheesecake. The main meals vary in price from €15 to €35.

- **Le Vieux harbor**: Located in Bastia's historic harbor, Le Vieux Port is noted for its delicious seafood and breathtaking vistas. Enjoy grilled fish, seafood platters, and tasty pasta while admiring the scenic surroundings. The main meals vary in price from €20 to €40.

- **A Nepita**: A Nepita is a wonderful restaurant located in the ancient area of Bastia. It serves typical Corsican delicacies such as veal medallions in chestnut sauce, Corsican-style cannelloni, and handmade desserts. The main meals vary in price from €15 to €30.

Restaurant Recommendations in Calvi

- L'Abri Cotier: This renowned seafood restaurant overlooks Calvi's port and is noted for its fresh catch of the day. Enjoy grilled fish, seafood platters, and local delicacies while relaxing on the waterfront. The main meals vary in price from €25 to €45.

- La Table de Bastien: La Table de Bastien, located in the heart of Calvi's citadel, provides a sophisticated dining experience with a cuisine that mixes Corsican and Mediterranean tastes. This restaurant offers a gourmet trip through the region's cuisine, from creative seafood dishes to exquisite grilled meats. The main meals vary in price from €30 to €55.

- Le Bistrot: Le Bistrot is a charming restaurant in Calvi's town center recognized for its friendly hospitality and traditional Corsican food. The cuisine includes Corsican cured meats, cheeses, and substantial stews produced with local ingredients. The main meals vary in price from €15 to €35.

Please keep in mind that the prices shown are estimates and may change based on the restaurant, season, and the foods purchased. When entering a restaurant, it's usually a good idea to browse the menu or question about rates.

Wine and Local Drinks

Corsica is well-known for its fine wines and native drinks, which represent the island's distinct terroir and traditional winemaking traditions. Here's a glance at the wine areas, varietals, and options for tasting excursions and vineyard visits in Corsica:

Corsican Wine Regions and Varietals

- Patrimonio: Located in the northwest corner of Corsica near Bastia, Patrimonio is the island's oldest and most prominent wine area. It is famous for its red wines produced from the Niellucciu grape, which yields powerful and fragrant wines with red fruit, herb, and spice characteristics. White wines made from Vermentinu grapes are very popular, giving a crisp and refreshing flavor with citrus and white floral overtones.

- Ajaccio: Ajaccio, located on Corsica's western coast near the capital city, is another noteworthy wine area. The Mediterranean environment benefits the vines here, resulting in wines with excellent structure and character. Sciaccarellu, the predominant red grape type, is noted for creating elegant and peppery wines with red fruit notes. Ajaccio also makes white wines from the Vermentino grape, which have a refreshing and mineral flavor.

- Figari: Located in southern Corsica, Figari is famous for its powerful red wines produced mostly from the local grape type, Sciaccarellu. These wines have a deep hue, intense aromas of blackberries and herbs, and robust tannins. Figari also makes white wines from Vermentino, with sharp acidity and citrus and tropical fruit aromas.

- Calvi: Located on Corsica's northwest coast, the Calvi wine area produces red, white, and rosé wines. Red wines are often created from a combination of Niellucciu, Sciaccarellu, and Grenache grapes, resulting in well-structured wines with rich fruit flavors and a touch of spice. White wines made from Vermentinu grapes have a lively acidity as well as lovely floral and fruity flavors.

Tasting Tours and Vineyard Visits

Consider engaging in tasting trips and visiting vineyards across the island to properly enjoy Corsican wines. Here are some possibilities to consider:

- **Wine excursions**: Join guided wine excursions through Corsica's gorgeous vineyards, where you can learn about the winemaking process and sample a range of wines. These excursions sometimes include stops at various wineries, enabling you to try a variety of styles and varietals.

- **Vineyard Visits**: Many Corsican wineries accept guests for tours and tastings. You may visit the vineyards, learn about the unique terroir of each location, and sample wines straight from the source. Some vineyards also provide educational opportunities, enabling you to learn more about Corsican wines.

- **Wine Festivals**: Throughout the year, Corsica offers many wine festivals that provide a joyous environment for tasting and celebrating local wines. Wine tastings, food pairings, live music, and cultural activities are common at these events, enabling you to immerse yourself in the island's wine culture.

- **Wine Cellars and Shops**: Wine cellars and stores may be found in towns and cities across Corsica, where you can explore and buy a broad variety of local wines. The expert staff can assist you in selecting the appropriate wines depending on your tastes, as well as providing information on various winemaking processes and varietals.

109

The price of Corsican wines varies based on the winery, the exact bottle, and the vintage. A bottle of Corsican wine may cost from

€10 to €40, with some higher-end wines costing more. The cost of tasting tours and vineyard visits may vary based on the degree of experience and the number of wineries visited. It's best to verify with the individual tour or vineyard for pricing information.

Exploring Corsican wines and drinks is a pleasant adventure that enables you to experience the island's distinct flavors and learn about the winemakers' enthusiasm. Whether you take a tasting tour, visit vineyards, or just enjoy a glass of Corsican wine at a local restaurant, the island's rich wine culture will amaze you.

Culinary Events and Festivals

Corsica is a gourmet haven, and the island celebrates its culinary history with a variety of festivals and events. These gourmet events provide a great experience for food and wine connoisseurs, presenting local delicacies and emphasizing area wines. Here are some prominent Corsican food festivals and events:

Chestnut Fairs

Corsica is famous for its chestnut orchards, and the island's chestnut celebrations honor this versatile staple. These festivities, which are usually held in the fall, highlight the many ways in which chestnuts are employed in Corsican cuisine. Here's what to expect:

- **Chestnut Tastings**: Sample roasted chestnuts, chestnut flour crepes, chestnut soup, and chestnut sweets such as castagnaccio (chestnut cake) and migliacci (chestnut pancake).

- **Local Products**: Explore stalls featuring local artisans and producers who offer a variety of chestnut products, such as chestnut honey, chestnut liqueur, chestnut preserves, and chestnut-based spreads.

- **Cultural Activities**: The chestnut celebrations are enhanced with live music, traditional dances, and cultural shows. You may also learn more about chestnut harvesting and processing by attending courses and demonstrations.

The Castagnedda di Corsica, celebrated in Bocognano in late October, is one of the most well-known chestnut festivals in Corsica. It draws people from all over the world who come to sample the tastes of Corsican chestnuts.

Seafood and Fishermen Festivals

Corsica has an abundance of fresh seafood due to its seaside position. Seafood and fisherman festivals allow visitors to commemorate the island's marine history while also sampling a variety of wonderful seafood meals. Here's what you may expect to see:

- **Seafood delicacies**: Enjoy grilled fish, seafood paella, bouillabaisse (fish stew), stuffed squid, and marinated anchovies, among other seafood delicacies. These festivities provide an excellent opportunity to sample the delicacies of the Mediterranean Sea.

- **Local fisherman's Market**: Visit the festival's busy fish markets, where local fisherman sells their catch of the day. Fresh fish, shellfish, and other seafood may be purchased straight from the fisherman to take home or eat on-site.

- **Culinary events**: Attend interesting culinary events where chefs demonstrate their expertise in producing seafood delicacies. These competitions often incorporate both traditional cuisine and creative innovations, giving the celebrations a competitive edge.

The Fête de la Mer in Bonifacio, celebrated in July, is a significant seafood festival in Corsica that celebrates the island's marine traditions and provides a feast of fresh seafood delicacies.

Wine and Gastronomy Events

Corsica's unique wine culture and gourmet legacy are honored throughout the year with wine and food festivals. These events highlight the different wines, local products, and culinary abilities of the island. Here are some things to look forward to:

- **Wine Tastings**: Sample the tastes of Corsican wines during tastings led by local winemakers. From crisp whites to strong reds, you may sample a broad selection of varietals and styles while being guided by an expert.

- **Gastronomic Delights**: Indulge in culinary experiences presented at these events to enjoy the marriage of food and wine. Renowned chefs and winemakers often combine to produce unique tasting menus that mix Corsican foods with Corsican wines.

- Vineyard tours: Some wine and gastronomy events include tours to vineyards and wineries, giving attendees a firsthand look at the winemaking process. You may tour the vineyards, learn about the production methods, and receive insights into the distinct terroir of Corsican wines.

Les Rencontres Vigneronnes, held in Calvi in August, is one of the most important wine festivals in Corsica. It brings together winemakers from all around the island, giving visitors the opportunity to sample a broad range of Corsican wines.

Please keep in mind that the dates and particular events may change from year to year, so it's best to check the most up-to-date information and event calendars to plan your visit appropriately.

Cultural Experiences

Corsica is a culturally diverse island with a long history that is commemorated via many art forms, music, and festivals. Immerse yourself in Corsica's lively cultural scene with these one-of-a-kind experiences

Music and Festivals in Corsica

Corsican music is recognized for its passionate melodies, powerful polyphonic singing, and strong ties to the island's history and customs. Experience the captivating sounds of Corsican music and take part in colorful events celebrating this distinct musical legacy.

Polyphonic Singing and Traditional Music

Polyphonic singing is a distinguishing feature of Corsican music. It consists of numerous voices harmonizing to produce a hauntingly beautiful and powerful sound. Traditional Corsican songs often deal with love, nature, and the island's history.

You may see polyphonic singing concerts in a variety of locations, including churches, cultural institutions, and outdoor venues, while visiting Corsica. These songs are passionately performed by local groups known as "cantu in paghjella," who captivate listeners with their melodious vocals and emotional performances.

Furthermore, indigenous musical instruments like as the cetera (Corsican lute), caramusa (bagpipes), and pifana (flute) are often incorporated in Corsican music, bringing depth and complexity to the tunes.

Music Festivals in Corsica

Throughout the year, Corsica holds a number of music events that allow visitors to experience the island's musical history as well as its modern music scene. These events bring together local and international performers, resulting in a lively environment full of live performances and cultural interchange.

- **Festival du Chant de Marin**: This famous maritime festival, held in Paimpol, Brittany (France), presents not just Corsican music but also traditional music from throughout the globe. It draws a varied spectrum of performers and provides a one-of-a-kind mix of cultures and musical genres.

- **Festival de Musique de Calvi**: Held in the ancient town of Calvi, this classical music festival features performances by famous orchestras, chamber groups, and soloists. The festival features both local and international artists and provides a diverse range of musical experiences.

- Les Nuits de la Guitare de Patrimonio: This guitar festival, held in the hamlet of Patrimonio, honors the beauty and flexibility of the instrument. It draws skilled guitarists from a variety of genres, such as classical, jazz, flamenco, and blues, resulting in a dynamic and compelling musical performance.

These are only a few examples of the many music events held in Corsica. The island's musical culture is always growing, with new festivals and events appearing every year, so it's best to check the most recent event schedules and plan your visit appropriately.

Please keep in mind that the dates and particular festivals may change from year to year, so it's best to check the most up-to-date information and event calendars to plan your visit appropriately.

Traditional Arts and Crafts

Corsica is recognized not just for its rich musical legacy, but also for its ancient crafts and art forms, which highlight the island's inventiveness and workmanship. Explore the traditional crafts and art activities listed here to have a better knowledge of Corsican culture.

Corsican Knife Making

Corsican knife manufacturing is a time-honored skill that entails a number of difficult stages in order to make high-quality blades. These practical and beautiful blades are often created by artisans using a blend of traditional and contemporary methods.

The manufacturing process starts with the selection of the best materials, such as high-quality steel for the blade and several kinds of wood for the handle. Skilled craftspeople shape and forge the blade with care, tempering it to produce ideal hardness and longevity. They then mold the handle to fit pleasantly in the hand, sometimes using indigenous Corsican woods like olive wood or juniper wood.

Decorated engravings, traditional Corsican emblems, or exquisite metallurgy are common on Corsican blades. These decorations enhance the completed knife's beauty and cultural importance.

Corsican knives vary in price according to the workmanship, materials used, and design complexity. A handmade Corsican knife may cost anywhere from €50 to €200 or more, depending on size and intricacy.

Ceramics and Pottery

Corsican pottery and ceramics are made using a blend of traditional methods and modern design features. Local clay and natural colors are used by artisans to produce one-of-a-kind creations that represent the island's natural beauty and cultural legacy.

The following stages are commonly included in the pottery-making process:

1. Preparation: To get the proper consistency and texture, the clay is carefully combined and prepared.

2. Shaping: Artists shape clay by hand or on a potter's wheel, using methods like coiling, pinching, and throwing to produce bowls, plates, vases, and figures.

3. To minimize breaking, the formed pottery is allowed to dry gently. Depending on the size and thickness of the object, this procedure might take several days or even weeks.

4. Firing: The dry pottery is fired at high temperatures in a kiln to turn the clay into a long-lasting ceramic substance. The fire process may also improve the appearance of the colors and glazes used on the pottery.

5. Decoration: After the pottery has been fired and cooled, artists use traditional processes to add glazes, paints, or ornamental features. Simple patterns to sophisticated hand-painted designs inspired by Corsican landscapes, flora, and animals may be seen in these decorations.

Corsican pottery and ceramics costs vary based on criteria such as size, design intricacy, and the renown of the artist or studio. Smaller pieces, such as bowls or cups, may cost between €20 and €50, while bigger and more highly adorned objects, such as vases or beautiful plates, might cost between €50 and €200 or more.

Art Galleries and Craft Work

When visiting Corsica, you may visit several art galleries and craft centers that highlight the ability and originality of the island's artists and craftspeople. These galleries include a wide variety of creative expressions, such as paintings, sculptures, jewelry, textiles, and other handcrafted items.

Prices for artworks and craft products at Corsican art galleries and craft centers may vary greatly based on the artist's renown, medium utilized, and size or intricacy of the piece. Paintings and sculptures by well-known artists might cost several hundred euros to several thousand euros or more. Handcrafted jewelry, textiles, and other craft items might cost between €20 and €200 or more, depending on the materials and methods used.

When buying artworks or handmade goods, it's crucial to ask individual artists or galleries about their pricing, since costs might vary greatly. Additionally, for individuals searching for more inexpensive mementos, some artists may provide more affordable solutions, such as prints or smaller copies. Exploring Corsica's traditional crafts and art forms enables you to admire the craftsmen's talent and passion while also purchasing one-of-a-kind and important artifacts that represent the island's cultural past.

Museums and historical sites

Corsica is rich in history, and various historical landmarks and museums provide insight into the island's past. To immerse yourself in Corsica's intriguing history, visit the following famous attractions:

Ajaccio's Napoleon Bonaparte Sites

Ajaccio, Napoleon Bonaparte's birthplace, is home to many landmarks linked with the famed French military and political leader. Here are some important places to visit:

- **Maison Bonaparte**: Tour the Maison Bonaparte, the ancestral house of the Bonaparte family and Napoleon Bonaparte's birthplace. Explore the museum on the interior, which shows the family's history as well as Napoleon's early life.

- **Place Foch and Napoleon Statue**: Take a stroll around Place Foch, a busy area in the center of Ajaccio that has a renowned statue of Napoleon Bonaparte. The monument honors the island's most well-known native son.

- **Ajaccio Cathedral**: Visit the Ajaccio Cathedral, which is where Napoleon Bonaparte was christened. Discover the historical importance of the gorgeous buildings.

- **Musée National de la Maison Bonaparte**: This museum, located near the Maison Bonaparte, has a collection of items and mementos relating to the Bonaparte family and Napoleon's life and career.

The Fesch Museum

The Fesch Museum in Ajaccio is well-known for its extensive collection of art and antiques. Here's what to anticipate from this cultural treasure:

- **Art Collection**: Outside of Italy, the Fesch Museum has one of the most comprehensive collections of Italian Renaissance paintings. Admire works by famous painters such as Botticelli, Titian, and Veronese.

- **Napoleon's Portraits**: The museum also has a major collection of Napoleon Bonaparte portraits, which provide insight into the renowned leader's image and depiction in art.

- **Antiquities**: Explore the museum's collection of sculptures, pottery, and jewelry from ancient Greece, Rome, and Egypt.

- Cultural Events: The Fesch Museum presents temporary exhibits and cultural events on occasion to enrich the visitor's experience and provide a wider perspective on art and history.

Corsican Resistance Museum

The Corsican Resistance Museum, situated in Corte, focuses light on Corsica's participation during WWII and its resistance to German rule. This famous historical museum has the following exhibits:

- **Exhibits and relics**: The museum showcases a variety of exhibits, relics, and papers that illustrate the history of Corsican resistance fighters, their techniques, and the problems they encountered throughout World War II.

- **Personal tales**: Learn about the strength and tenacity of people who played important roles in the resistance movement via their personal tales.

- **Interactive exhibits**: To give a thorough knowledge of Corsica's resistance activities, the museum utilizes interactive exhibits, video presentations, and immersive experiences.

- **Educational Programs**: The Corsican Resistance Museum provides educational programs and guided tours for visitors of all ages, giving it a great place to study and ponder.

Corsica's historical sites and museums have varying prices. Adult entrance to Maison Bonaparte costs roughly €7, whereas adult access to the Fesch Museum costs around €8. The Corsican Resistance Museum normally charges an adult admission price of about €6. Prices are subject to change, so check the official websites or contact the museums directly for the most up-to-date information.

Visiting these historical landmarks and museums in Corsica helps you to have a better grasp of the island's history and appreciate its rich cultural heritage. From discovering Napoleon Bonaparte's ancestors in Ajaccio to enjoying the art collection at the Fesch Museum and learning about Corsica's resistance during WWII, these sites provide an enthralling tour through history.

Shopping and Local Markets

Immerse yourself in the vivid ambiance of Corsica's local markets and treat yourself to a one-of-a-kind shopping experience. Here are some prominent markets and shopping ideas to help you make the most of your visit:

Ajaccio Market

Ajaccio, Corsica's main city, has a lively market with a broad variety of local goods and delicacies. Here's what to anticipate from Ajaccio Market:

Ajaccio Market is well-known for its fresh food, which includes fruits, vegetables, herbs, and spices. Explore the vibrant booths and sample the flavors of locally farmed products.

Corsica is well-known for its handmade cheeses and charcuterie. Explore the assortment of cured meats, like lonzu and coppa, and sample a range of savory cheeses, such as brocciu and tomme.

- **Corsican Specialties**: Sample Corsican specialties such as honey, olive oil, jams, and preserves. These dishes reflect the rich culinary traditions of the island and make ideal keepsakes or presents.

- **handmade things**: Ajaccio Market also sells handmade things such as ceramics, textiles, jewelry, and traditional

Corsican knives. These homemade pieces highlight the island's particular workmanship and make for memorable souvenirs.

Bastia Market

Bastia, in Corsica's northeastern corner, has a bustling market that represents the city's genuine appeal. At Bastia Market, look for the following highlights:

- **Fish and Seafood Market**: As a seaside city, Bastia is well-known for its fresh seafood. You'll discover an outstanding range of fish, shellfish, and other coastal pleasures at the market. Enjoy the tastes of the Mediterranean while eating the catch of the day.

- **Corsican delicacies** include cured meats, sausages, and regional specialities such as figatellu, a classic Corsican pig sausage. Taste the distinct tastes and fragrances that distinguish the island's cuisine.

- **Artisanal Crafts**: In addition to woven baskets, pottery, leather goods, and ornamental items, Bastia Market sells a variety of locally created things. These handmade items represent the traditional craftsmanship of the island and are valuable mementos.

Shopping Tips for Local Products

Keep the following ideas in mind while buying for Corsican products:

- **Authenticity and Quality**: Look for labels or signs of local origin to confirm the authenticity and quality of the things you buy. AOC (Appellation d'Origine Contrôlée) for wines and AOP (Appellation d'Origine Protégée) for certain food items are common designations for Corsican goods.

- Market Days and Hours: Corsican markets are normally open on particular days and hours. It's a good idea to verify the local timetables ahead of time so you can arrange your visit properly.

- Bargaining: In Corsican marketplaces, bargaining is uncommon. Prices are frequently set, particularly for food goods. However, it is always acceptable to ask sellers questions and participate in discussions to learn more about their goods and customs.

- Supporting Local Producers: Buying from local markets directly benefits Corsican producers and craftsmen, enabling you to contribute to the island's economy while also preserving its cultural history. Take advantage of the chance to interact with locals and learn about their crafts and customs.

Local market pricing might vary based on the items and providers. Fresh produce costs are typically competitive, while the price of cheeses, charcuterie, and local delicacies varies according to the nature and quality of the items. The cost of handcrafted objects varies greatly based on their intricacy and the materials utilized. It is advised that you visit many booths, compare costs, and choose things that fit your tastes and budget.

Exploring Corsica's local markets allows you to not only buy unique and original items but also to immerse yourself in the island's lively culture and connect with its people. Enjoy the vibrant atmosphere, sample the delicacies, and take a bit of Corsica's rich culinary and cultural legacy home with you.

Packing Essentials

When it comes to packing for your trip to Corsica, it's important to be prepared for the varied activities and weather conditions you may encounter. To help you organize your packing list, here are the essential categories and items you should consider:

Clothing and Footwear

- **Lightweight and breathable clothing**: Pack a variety of clothing options suitable for warm weather, including t-shirts, shorts, skirts, and dresses. Opt for breathable fabrics like cotton or linen to stay cool and comfortable.

- **Long-sleeved shirts and lightweight sweaters**: Corsica's weather can be unpredictable, especially in the mountainous regions. Pack a few long-sleeved shirts and lightweight sweaters to layer when the temperature drops or for protection against sunburn.

- **Pants or hiking trousers**: If you plan on hiking or participating in outdoor activities, pack a pair of comfortable and durable pants or hiking trousers. These will provide protection from scratches, bugs, and the sun.

- **Waterproof and windproof jacket**: Corsica experiences occasional rain showers, even during the summer months. Bring a lightweight, waterproof, and windproof jacket to stay dry and shielded from the elements.

- **Sturdy walking or hiking shoes**: Invest in a good pair of walking or hiking shoes to navigate Corsica's diverse terrain.

Choose comfortable shoes with a strong grip and ankle support for stability during hikes.

- Sandals or flip-flops: Pack a pair of sandals or flip-flops for strolling along the beach or for casual outings.

- Swimwear and beach towel: Corsica is famous for its beautiful beaches and clear waters. Don't forget to pack your swimwear and a lightweight beach towel for sunbathing and swimming

- Hat, sunglasses, and sunscreen: Protect yourself from the sun's rays by packing a wide-brimmed hat, sunglasses with UV protection, and a high SPF sunscreen. These will help prevent sunburn and keep you comfortable under the sun.

Outdoor Gear and Equipment
- Daypack or backpack: A small daypack or backpack is essential for carrying your daily essentials, such as water, snacks, sunscreen, a map, and a camera.

- Water bottle or hydration system: Staying hydrated is crucial, especially during outdoor activities. Bring a reusable water bottle or consider a hydration system with a built-in water bladder for easy access to water.

- Insect repellent and mosquito net: Corsica has its fair share of insects, especially in rural areas. Pack insect repellent to ward off mosquitoes and other bugs. If you plan to camp, a mosquito net can provide a peaceful night's sleep.

- Portable power bank: Keep your electronic devices charged on the go by bringing a portable power bank. This will ensure you can capture memories with your camera or stay connected with your smartphone.

125

- Travel adapter: Corsica uses the standard European two-pin plug sockets, so if you're traveling from a country with different plug types, bring a travel adapter to charge your devices.

- Portable Bluetooth speaker: If you enjoy listening to music while relaxing on the beach or having a picnic, a portable Bluetooth speaker can enhance your experience.

- Dry bag or waterproof pouch: Protect your valuable items from water damage by packing a dry bag or waterproof pouch. This is especially useful for water activities, such as kayaking or boat trips.

Toiletries and Personal Items

- Toiletries: Pack travel-sized toiletries, including shampoo, conditioner, body wash, toothpaste, and a toothbrush. Remember to bring any necessary medications, including prescriptions.

- First aid kit: Prepare a basic first aid kit with essentials such as band-aids, antiseptic ointment, pain relievers, insect bite cream, and any personal medications.

- Travel towel and toiletry bag: Consider bringing a quick-drying and compact travel towel, along with a toiletry bag to keep your items organized.

Miscellaneous

- Travel documents: Carry your passport, identification, travel insurance documents, and any necessary visas or permits in a secure travel document organizer.

- **Cash and cards**: It's recommended to have a combination of cash and cards (debit or credit) for your expenses. While cards are widely accepted, having some cash on hand is useful for smaller businesses or remote areas.

- **Guidebooks and maps**: Bring guidebooks or download digital maps and travel apps to help you navigate Corsica's attractions and find useful information.

- **Language guide**: While many locals in Corsica speak French, it can be helpful to have a pocket-sized language guide or a translation app to communicate basic phrases.

- **Travel locks**: Ensure the security of your belongings by packing travel locks for your luggage and backpack.

Other electronic gadgets

- **Smartphone**: Your smartphone will likely be your go-to device for communication, navigation, and capturing memories. Make sure to bring your charger or a portable power bank to keep it charged throughout the day.

- **Camera**: If you're passionate about photography, consider bringing a dedicated camera to capture stunning landscapes and moments during your trip. Don't forget spare batteries, memory cards, and any necessary camera accessories.

- Universal Travel Adapter: Corsica uses the standard European two-pin plug sockets, so if you're traveling from a country with a different plug type, bring a universal travel adapter to charge your electronic devices.

- **Headphones**: Whether you're listening to music on the beach or enjoying audio guides during museum visits, a pair of headphones will enhance your experience. Choose wireless headphones for convenience.

- **E-reader or Tablet**: If you're an avid reader, consider bringing an e-reader or tablet to enjoy your favorite books without the added weight of physical copies. It can also serve as a versatile device for browsing the internet, watching movies, or organizing your travel itinerary.

- **Portable Wi-Fi Hotspot:** If you require constant internet access, consider renting or purchasing a portable Wi-Fi hotspot. This will allow you to stay connected and access online maps, travel apps, and stay in touch with loved ones.

- **Travel Apps**: Download relevant travel apps before your trip to Corsica. These can include navigation apps like Google Maps, translation apps, weather apps, and travel guides for quick access to information.

Remember to pack these electronic essentials securely and ensure they are easily accessible during your journey. Additionally, be mindful of any travel restrictions or regulations regarding the use of electronic devices in certain locations or modes of transportation.

The prices of electronic items can vary greatly depending on the brand, model, and features. It's advisable to compare prices online, check for any promotions or discounts, and consider the specific requirements and preferences that suit your needs.

Remember to check the baggage allowance and weight restrictions of your airline before packing, as they may vary. Additionally, consider the duration of your trip and the activities you plan to participate in when determining the number of items to pack.

With this comprehensive packing list, you'll be well-prepared for your adventure in Corsica, ready to enjoy the beautiful landscapes, outdoor activities, and cultural experiences the island has to offer.

Customs and Etiquette

Social Customs and Greetings

- Greetings: When greeting someone in Corsica, it is traditional to shake hands. Friends and acquaintances may also exchange cheek kisses, beginning with the left cheek.

- **Politeness**: Corsicans place a high priority on courtesy and respect in their dealings. When entering or leaving a business, restaurant, or other public location, it is necessary to say "Bonjour" (hello) and "Au revoir" (goodbye) when entering or leaving a shop, restaurant, or any public place. Saying "S'il vous plaît" (please) and "Merci" (thank you) is also appreciated in daily interactions.

- **Personal Space**: Corsicans cherish their personal space, so keep a reasonable distance while chatting with people. Unless you have a strong connection with the individual, avoid standing too near or touching.

- **Language**: Corsica's official language is French, although Corsican, a Romance language, is also widely spoken. Although it is not necessary, learning a few simple Corsican words or pleasantries is a kind gesture.

- **Dress Code**: Corsicans dress comfortably but modestly. It is customary to dress more modestly while visiting holy places, covering shoulders and knees.

Tipping and Service Charges

- **Tipping:** In Corsica, tipping is not obligatory but is appreciated for good service. If you're satisfied with the service you received at a restaurant or café, you can leave a small tip. A typical tip is around 5-10% of the total bill.

- **Service Charges**: A service fee (service compris) may be added to the bill at certain establishments. Tipping is not required in such instances, but you may still leave some extra coins as a token of gratitude.

- **Round-Up**: If no service fee is included, it is customary to round up the amount while paying. If your bill is 18 euros, for example, you may round it up to 20 euros.

- **Hotel personnel**: If hotel personnel, such as bellboys or cleaning, give great service, it is traditional to tip them. A few euros as a gratuity is acceptable.

- **Taxi Drivers**: Tipping taxi drivers is not mandatory, but it's common to round up the fare or add a small tip as a token of appreciation.

It's worth noting that, although tipping is appreciated, it's not mandatory in Corsica. The most essential thing is to be kind, respectful, and grateful for the assistance you get.

Useful Phrases and Vocabulary

9.5.1 Basic French Phrases for Travelers:

- Hello: Bonjour (bohn-zhoor)

- Goodbye: Au revoir (oh ruh-vwahr)

- Yes: Oui (wee)

- No: Non (nohn)

- Please: S'il vous plaît (seel voo pleh)

- Thank you: Merci (mehr-see)

- You're welcome: De rien (duh ree-ehn)

- Excuse me: Excusez-moi (ehk-skoo-zay mwa)

- Sorry: Pardon (pahr-dohn)

- I don't understand: Je ne comprends pas (zhuh nuh kohm-prahn pah)

- Do you speak English?: Parlez-vous anglais ? (pahr-ley voo ahn-gley)

Corsican Language Phrases
- Hello: Bonghjornu (boh-nyor-nu)

- Goodbye: Arrivederci (ah-ree-veh-dehr-chee)

- Thank you: Grazie (graht-see)

- Please: Per piacè (pehr pyah-cheh)

- Yes: È (eh)

- No: Nò (noh)

- Excuse me: Scusate (skoo-zah-teh)

- I'm sorry: Mi dispiace (mee dees-pyah-cheh)

131

- Can you help me?: Mi pò aiutà ? (mee poh a-yoo-tah)

- Where is...?: Unde si trova...? (oon-deh see troh-vah)

It's worth noting that while French is the official language of Corsica, Corsican, a Romance language, is also widely spoken. The Corsican language has regional variations, and some older generations may primarily speak Corsican. Learning a few basic phrases in both French and Corsican can be appreciated by the locals and enhance your travel experience in Corsica.

CHAPTER FIVE
Corsica with Kids
Family-Friendly Activities

- **Nature Exploration**: Corsica provides several possibilities for children to engage in nature exploration. Guided nature excursions or short treks in locations like the Scandola Nature Reserve or the Aiguilles de Bavella are ideal. Encourage children to study the island's various flora and animals, find unusual rock formations, and learn about its natural beauty.

- **Beach Fun**: Corsica has several family-friendly beaches with calm waves and services. Aside from swimming and constructing sandcastles, youngsters may enjoy beach volleyball, snorkeling, or even a relaxing boat trip around the coast. Rondinara Beach, Calvi Beach, and Tonnara Beach are among the most popular beaches for families.

- **Adventure Parks**: Visit Corsica's adventure parks for some adrenaline-pumping excitement. Rope courses, tree-top experiences, and zip-lining are among the fascinating activities available at these parks. Acqua Vanua, situated near Ghisonaccia, is a noteworthy park that provides exciting rides and water-based activities appropriate for children of all ages.

- **Animal Encounters**: Corsica includes animal shelters and farms where children may engage with a variety of animals. See animals up close at sites like Parc Animalier et Exotique de la Haute-Corse, where you can see deer, llamas, wallabies, and more. Some farms also allow visitors to feed and pet animals, which is both instructive and amusing.

Child-Friendly Beaches

- **Palombaggia Beach**: Located near Porto-Vecchio, Palombaggia Beach is noted for its magnificent beauty and child-friendly qualities. It has shallow seas, moderate slopes, and fine sand, making it suitable for children. The beach is flanked by pine trees, which provide shade on hot summer days.

- **Santa Giulia Beach**: Santa Giulia Beach, located in the Gulf of Porto-Vecchio, is another wonderful alternative for families. The shallow, blue seas are ideal for small children to splash about in, and the soft sandy beach is ideal for sandcastle construction. The beach also offers water sports activities for older children and teens.

- **Saleccia Beach**: Although more remote and difficult to reach, Saleccia Beach rewards tourists with a serene and pristine atmosphere. The tranquil and clear waves, as well as the immaculate sandy beach, make it ideal for families looking for a more isolated beach experience. To get to Saleccia Beach, consider taking a boat ride or a 4x4 tour.

Attractions and Theme Parks

- **Corsica Aventure Park**: Corsica Aventure Park, located in Porto-Vecchio, is a popular location for families looking for adventurous activities. The park offers a variety of tree-top obstacle courses, zip lines, and climbing activities for people of all ages. It's a fantastic location for youngsters to test themselves and enjoy outdoor experiences in a safe setting.

- **Cupulatta Tortoise Park**: Located near Ajaccio, Cupulatta Tortoise Park is a one-of-a-kind attraction where children can learn about and watch several types of tortoises and turtles.

The park supports conservation and educational programs, making it an excellent choice for families interested in animals and ecology.

Kid-Friendly Accommodation

Resorts: Many Corsican resorts cater to families and provide a variety of services and activities for children. These resorts often feature kids' clubs, pools, playgrounds, and scheduled entertainment activities for people of all ages. Club Med Cargèse, Les Jardins de la Madrague, and Résidence Dary are all excellent family resorts.

- **Self-Catering Apartments or Villas**: For families, renting a self-catering apartment or villa might be a convenient option. It allows you to make meals based on your family's tastes and provides additional room for youngsters to play and rest. Look for lodgings with outside facilities for children, such as gardens or terraces.

- **Family-Friendly Hotels**: Many Corsican hotels provide family rooms or suites with features like as cribs, high chairs, and additional beds. Some hotels also include kids' meals, childcare services, and entertainment alternatives including gaming rooms or kids' clubs. Consider staying in the Hotel San Carlu Citadelle, the Hotel Calvi, or the Hotel Capo d'Orto.

When visiting Corsica with children, it is essential to choose activities and lodgings that are appropriate for their age and interests. Plan ahead of time to ensure you have enough time to appreciate each activity without feeling rushed. Remember to bring sunscreen, hats, bug repellant, and snacks to keep your children comfortable and energetic throughout the day.

Corsica's Nightlife

Please accept my apologies for not giving adequate information. Here's a more in-depth look of Corsica's nightlife:

Nightclubs and Bars

Corsica has a wide variety of pubs and nightclubs, so there's something for everyone. Consider the following common alternatives:

- **Ajaccio**: Ajaccio has a variety of active pubs and clubs distributed across the city. Rue Bonaparte and Rue Cardinal Fesch are especially well-known for their lively nightlife. Cocktails and a relaxing environment are popular at Le Café de la Place and Le Barfly. Le Garage and L'Indigo are two famous nightclubs for individuals looking for a dynamic partying experience.

- **Porto-Vecchio**: Porto-Vecchio is well-known for its vibrant nightlife, particularly during the summer months. The primary attractions are the Old Port and the districts around Place de la République. Via Notte, a big outdoor nightclub, and Le Piazzetta, a contemporary pub with live music, are two popular locations.

- **Calvi**: Calvi has a thriving nightlife scene, especially during the summer months. Near the marina, the Quai Landry neighborhood is densely packed with pubs and clubs. La Vinoteca, with its large wine list, is an excellent choice for a relaxing evening. For a livelier experience, visit Le B52 or Le Plaza, both of which are recognized for their vibrant environment and music.

Live Music and Entertainment

Corsica has a variety of music venues where you may see live performances. The Palais Fesch in Ajaccio often organizes classical music events, while Le Référendum is a popular venue for local bands and new performers. Les Baléares in Calvi is well-known for its live music performances, which include rock, jazz, and reggae.

- **Festivals**: Corsica hosts several music festivals throughout the year. The Calvi on the Rocks festival, held in July, features electronic and indie music on the beach. The Porto Latino festival in Saint-Florent celebrates world music and Latin rhythms. These festivals attract renowned artists and provide a lively and memorable experience.

Cultural Evening Events

- **Corsican Polyphonic Singing:** Corsica is well-known for its distinct polyphonic singing history. Performances are often held in churches, cultural institutions, or specialized locations. - Theater and Dance: Corsica's theater and dance scene provides a variety of productions, including plays, ballets, and modern dance acts, and is a must-see for those interested in Corsican music. The Teatro di a Piazza in Ajaccio and the TeatrEuropa in Bastia are famous places to see theatrical and dance acts.

Corsica's nightlife is vibrant, however, it's crucial to realize that the intensity varies based on the season and location. Coastal towns and tourism destinations are often more dynamic during the summer months, with various activities and a bustling environment. In contrast, certain inland regions may provide a more tranquil and peaceful atmosphere.

During your visit, it's a good idea to check local event listings and ask locals for ideas, since there may be special performances, themed evenings, or cultural activities going on. Also, take in mind that the opening hours and entire ambiance might vary between weekdays and weekends, with weekends often being busier.

Prices might vary based on the establishment and region. Drinks at pubs and nightclubs are generally similar to other European destinations. To prevent unpleasant surprises, examine the menu or enquire about costs before ordering.

Finally, while enjoying Corsica's nightlife, it's essential to drink sensibly and be safe. Plan your transportation ahead of time, consider designated drivers, or utilize taxi services to securely travel to and from your location.

Where to Buy Fashion and Design wears

Corsica has a wide range of possibilities for fashion and design aficionados. Corsica offers something for everyone, whether you're seeking for fashionable apparel, accessories, or distinctive home décor. Here are two categories to explore.

Fashion Boutiques in Corsica

Corsican Fashion Boutiques include a mix of local and worldwide brands, as well as Corsican designers' creativity and flair. Here are some suggested locations:

- Ajaccio

- **Rue Fesch**: Ajaccio's vibrant strip is famed for its stylish businesses. There are a variety of shops selling stylish apparel, footwear, and accessories. Look for both local and worldwide names, as well as boutique businesses featuring Corsican designers' work.

Porto Vecchio
- **Rue Général Leclerc**: This street in Porto-Vecchio is a hotspot for high-end fashion retailers. Designer apparel, swimwear, footwear, and accessories are available here. Explore the neighborhood for worldwide luxury brands as well as local designers catering to a variety of styles and interests.

- Bastia
- **Rue Napoléon**: Bastia's pedestrian streets, such as Rue Napoléon, are home to a mix of well-known fashion stores and independent businesses. You'll discover a wide range of wardrobe selections, from casual to more professional.

Home Design and Decor Stores
Corsica also has a variety of design and home decor boutiques where you may buy unique and fashionable products for your house. Take a look at the following locations:

- Bonifacio Aquino
- **Rue des Deux Empereurs and Rue du Palais:** These streets in Bonifacio's lovely town are dotted with attractive stores selling home design products. To add a bit of Corsican flair to your house, look for locally created pottery, fabrics, and decorative objects.

- Calvi

- Rue Clemenceau and Rue de la Porte Genoise: Visit these Calvi streets to find design and home décor boutiques that provide a mix of modern and classic designs. You'll discover one-of-a-kind home furniture, lighting, fabrics, and decorative artifacts.

- Corte

- Streets around the citadel: Explore the streets surrounding the citadel in the medieval town of Corte to uncover artisanal workshops and businesses displaying locally manufactured design and home décor goods. To add a touch of Corsican workmanship to your room, look for handcrafted furniture, delicate ceramics, and fabrics.

Prices for fashion and design goods in Corsica might vary based on the brand, quality, and originality of the products. High-end boutiques and designer stores will have higher price ranges by definition, but smaller boutiques and craft shops may have more accessible selections. It's a good idea to shop about, compare costs, and think about the quality and workmanship of the products you're interested in.

Explore Corsica's fashion and design scene to discover the right complements to your wardrobe and home décor!

Corsica's Hidden Gems

Corsica is full of hidden treasures, such as quiet beaches and secret coves that provide a calm and untouched coastal experience. These hidden jewels provide a chance to get away from the throng and explore the island's natural beauty in a more intimate environment.

Remote and Secluded Beaches

- Plage de Saleccia: Located in the Agriates Desert in Corsica's northwest, this gorgeous beach is only accessible by boat or a difficult off-road trek. It is a wonderfully hidden paradise, with blue lakes, fine white sand, and surrounding dunes.

- Plage de Roccapina: Located near Bonifacio in southern Corsica, this hidden treasure provides a gorgeous setting with golden beaches, blue waves, and a stunning rock formation like a lion laying down.

- Plage de Nonza: Located in the northern Corsican town of Nonza, this pebble beach offers spectacular views of the turquoise sea and the area's characteristic black tower. It's a hidden treasure noted for its raw beauty and one-of-a-kind vibe.

Hidden Coves and Swimming Holes

- Calanques de Piana: The Calanques de Piana are a collection of magnificent rocky coves and natural swimming holes located near Porto on Corsica's western coast. These hidden treasures provide a private location to cool down in crystal-clear waters surrounded by stunning red granite cliffs.

- Gorges de la Restonica: The Gorges de la Restonica, located near Corte in central Corsica, is a beautiful natural marvel with tumbling waterfalls and crystalline pools. It's a great area for trekking and exploring secret swimming holes hidden among stunning surroundings.

To find these hidden treasures, it's frequently essential to go off the main route and explore Corsica's lesser-known locations. Some may need more work and preparation, such as trekking or driving off-road vehicles to reach more distant sites. Others, such as Plage de Saleccia, may only be reached by boat or via guided trips.

Before seeing these hidden treasures, it's critical to learn about their locations and accessibility. Consult local guides, tourist information centers, or internet resources for the most up-to-date information on how to safely access these remote locations.

Discovering Corsica's secret beaches and coves enables you to appreciate the natural beauty of the island in a more personal and quiet setting. To protect these hidden jewels for future visitors, remember to respect the environment, observe any rules in existence, and leave no trace.

Explore the hidden seaside jewels of Corsica and make amazing moments in these quiet paradises!

Charming Hilltop Villages

Corsica is recognized for its picturesque hilltop villages as well as its gorgeous beaches and natural settings. These charming hilltop villages provide a look into Corsica's rich history, traditional architecture, and stunning vistas. Here are three picturesque hilltop villages worth visiting:

Nonza

Nonza, located on Corsica's northwest coast, is a one-of-a-kind hilltop town that captivates tourists with its spectacular scenery and rich history. Here is all you need to know about Nonza:

Nonza is located on the Cap Corse peninsula, with views of the Mediterranean Sea. It's around 20 kilometers northwest of Bastia.

- **Historic Charm**: Nonza is famed for its medieval charm, which is distinguished by small lanes, stone homes, and the Tour de Nonza, a remarkable Genoese tower. The ancient ambience and maintained buildings of the village provide a wonderful aura.

- **Black Pebble Beach**: Nonza's beautiful black pebble beach is one of its most noteworthy characteristics. The contrast between the black stones and the blue water provides a one-of-a-kind and enthralling image. Visitors may enjoy the scenery by taking a leisurely walk along the beach.

Pigna

Pigna, located in northern Corsica's Balagne area, is a picturesque hilltop town known for its artistic history and traditional Corsican culture. Here's what to anticipate when you visit Pigna:

- Location: Pigna is located 9 kilometers southeast of Calvi, inland. Because of its lofty location, it provides panoramic views of the surrounding landscape and shoreline.

Pigna is well-known for its thriving creative community and traditional handicraft. There are various craftsmen, studios, and galleries in the town where tourists may explore and buy locally manufactured items like ceramics, jewelry, and traditional musical instruments.

- **Cultural Events**: Throughout the year, Pigna holds a variety of cultural events, including music festivals and art exhibits.

These events highlight the village's rich artistic tradition and provide a unique chance to immerse yourself in Corsican culture.

Sant'Antonino

Sant'Antonino, located on a hill in northern Corsica, is regarded as one of the most beautiful settlements on the island. Here are some facts about Sant'Antonino:

- **Location**: Sant'Antonino lies about 10 kilometers southeast of Île-Rousse in the Balagne area. Its lofty location provides amazing views of the surrounding countryside and beaches.

Sant'Antonino is a well-preserved medieval town with small cobblestone lanes, stone buildings, and historic defenses. The architectural legacy and natural splendor of the town make it a popular destination for travelers looking for a genuine Corsican experience.

- **Historical Importance**: Sant'Antonino is one of France's "Plus Beaux Villages" (Most Beautiful Villages) and has a rich history. Explore the historic attractions of the hamlet, such as the 9th-century Baroque Church of St. Antoine and the ruins of the medieval fortress.

It is best to have a vehicle or use public transit to get to these picturesque hilltop settlements. Each hamlet has its own distinct personality and charms, so it's worthwhile to spend some time exploring their streets, admiring the scenery, and soaking up the local ambiance.

Visiting Nonza, Pigna, and Sant'Antonino gives you a taste of Corsica's intriguing history, architectural splendor, and traditional way of life. These hilltop towns provide a calm respite as well as a chance to immerse yourself in the true charm of the island.

Explore Corsica's lovely hilltop villages and make lasting memories in these magical surroundings!

Remote Mountain Retreats

Corsica is recognized for its breathtaking natural settings, and its secluded mountain resorts provide a peaceful respite for nature lovers and adventure enthusiasts. Here are three distant mountain valleys to visit:

Asco Valley

The Asco Valley, located in northern Corsica, is a quiet and scenic mountain getaway with spectacular scenery and a variety of outdoor activities. Here's what you should know about Asco Valley:

- **Location**: The Asco Valley is located in the Corsican Alps, some 70 kilometers northwest of Bastia. It is accessible by automobile through the D147 route.

The region is known for its Rocky Mountains, lush woods, and crystal-clear rivers. The Asco River runs through the valley, providing stunning falls and natural pools ideal for swimming and picnics.

- **Outdoor Activities**: The Asco Valley is an outdoor enthusiast's dream. It has hiking, mountain biking, rock climbing, canyoning, and river rafting options. This valley also has the famed Monte Cinto, Corsica's tallest summit.

Restonica Valley

The Restonica Valley, located in central Corsica, is a lonely and picturesque mountain hideaway famed for its breathtaking scenery and unspoiled natural surroundings. Here's what to anticipate if you go to Restonica Valley:

- **Location**: The Restonica Valley is around 70 kilometers southeast of Corte, Corsica's old capital. It is accessible by automobile through the D623 route.

- **Spectacular Scenery**: The valley's towering granite peaks, thick pine woods, and crystal-clear alpine streams set it apart. The Restonica River flows through the valley, creating various natural pools and waterfalls suitable for swimming and resting.

- **Hiking & Trekking**: Hikers and nature enthusiasts flock to the Restonica Valley. Several well-marked routes lead to breathtaking vistas, alpine lakes, and mountain passes. Hiking routes from the valley lead to the famed Lake Melu and Lake Capitello.

Vallée de la Solenzara
The Vallée de la Solenzara, located on Corsica's eastern coast, is a lonely and pristine mountain valley famed for its rough beauty and outdoor sports. Here are some facts about the Vallée de la Solenzara:

- **Location**: The Vallée de la Solenzara is around 90 kilometers south of Bastia. It is accessible by automobile through the T10 highway.

- **Natural Wonders**: The valley is known for its steep gorges, high cliffs, and clear rivers. The Solenzara River runs through the valley, providing swimming, kayaking, and canyoning options. The nearby mountains offer a fantastic background for outdoor activities.

- **Outdoor Adventures**: The Vallée de la Solenzara is an outdoor enthusiast's dream. Hiking, rock climbing, mountain biking, and horseback riding are among the sports available. Climbers go to the adjacent Bavella Massif, which provides amazing views of the surrounding surroundings.

These secluded mountain getaways provide a one-of-a-kind chance to reconnect with nature, enjoy tranquillity, and participate in a variety of outdoor activities. The Asco Valley, Restonica Valley, and Vallée de la Solenzara provide amazing experiences in Corsica's Rocky Mountains, whether you're looking for adventure or just want to observe the natural beauty.

Please keep in mind that it is essential to be equipped with adequate outdoor clothing, have a thorough awareness of the terrain and weather conditions, and follow safety standards while visiting these remote regions to guarantee a safe and pleasurable trip.

Gorges de la Restonica

The Gorges de la Restonica are a beautiful natural marvel in central Corsica's Restonica Valley. Here's what you should know about this buried treasure:

- **Location:** The Gorges de la Restonica are around ten kilometers southeast of Corte. It is accessible by automobile through the D623 route.

- **Spectacular Scenery:** The Restonica River built the gorge, which is a narrow and stunning canyon. Towering granite

148

cliffs, rich flora, and crystal-clear blue seas define it. The gorge's panoramic grandeur is simply magnificent, and there are several picture possibilities.

- **Hiking and Nature Trails**: Hikers and nature enthusiasts will adore the Gorges de la Restonica. Several well-marked hiking paths wind through the canyon, providing chances to explore the surrounding landscapes, uncover hidden waterfalls, and take in panoramic views of the valley.

Lake Nino

Lake Nino is a beautiful alpine lake in the midst of Corsica's Regional Natural Park. Here's all you need to know about this buried treasure:

Lake Nino is located in the highlands of central Corsica, some 20 kilometers northwest of Corte. It is accessible through a moderate hiking trek.

- **Natural Beauty:** The lake is bordered by craggy hills and set among lush meadows, providing a magnificent alpine environment. The lake's quiet waters mirror the surrounding mountains, creating a pleasant and serene ambiance.

- **trekking and Wildlife:** The Lake Nino path is a famous trekking route that highlights the beauty of the Corsican highlands. Along the route, you may come across a variety of species, including wild horses, sheep, and birds. During the summer, the region is also famed for its vivid wildflowers.

Cascades des Anglais

The Cascades des Anglais, often known as the English Waterfalls, are a hidden jewel in the Corsican countryside. Here's all you need to know about this natural marvel:

- **Location**: Cascades des Anglais lies in the northern Corsican municipality of San-Gavino-di-Tenda. It is accessible by automobile through the D39 route.

- **Majestic Waterfalls**: A series of cascades and waterfalls pour over a gorgeous rocky valley at the location. The water falls into crystal ponds, providing a pleasant and attractive environment. The cascades are surrounded by rich flora, which adds to the area's charm.

- Swimming and Picnicking: Cascades des Anglais is a beautiful place to swim and picnic. You may cool yourself in the natural pools and have a picnic on the river's banks. It's a great spot to unwind and relax in nature.

These natural beauties off the usual route provide an opportunity to discover Corsica's hidden gems and connect with its natural beauty. The Gorges de la Restonica, Lake Nino, and Cascades des Anglais give amazing experiences in Corsica's natural surroundings, whether you're looking for adventure, peace, or magnificent scenery.

Travel Itineraries

A detailed 7 days itinerary

Day 1: Arrive in Bastia

- Explore the Old Port and visit the Terra Nova Citadel.

- Cost: Accommodation in Bastia can range from $50 to $150 per night, depending on your preferences and budget.

Day 2: Scenic Drive to Calvi

- Take a leisurely drive along the coast to Calvi, stopping at beautiful viewpoints along the way.

- Spend the afternoon exploring the historic center of Calvi and visit the Citadel.

- Cost: Accommodation in Calvi can range from $80 to $200 per night.

Day 3: Beach Day in Porto-Vecchio

- Travel to Porto-Vecchio and spend the day relaxing on the beautiful beaches of Palombaggia and Santa Giulia.

- Enjoy water activities such as swimming and snorkeling.

- Cost: Accommodation in Porto-Vecchio can range from $100 to $300 per night.

Day 4: Discover Bonifacio

- Explore the ancient town of Bonifacio, known for its medieval citadel and stunning cliffside location.

- Visit the King of Aragon's Stairway, the historic sites, and enjoy panoramic views of the sea.

- Cost: Accommodation in Bonifacio can range from $100 to $300 per night.

Day 5: Hiking in the Restonica Valley

- Drive to Corte and hike in the Restonica Valley, exploring the beautiful natural surroundings and waterfalls.

- Enjoy a picnic lunch in nature.

- Cost: Accommodation in Corte can range from $70 to $150 per night.

Day 6: Ajaccio and Napoleon Bonaparte

- Visit Ajaccio, the birthplace of Napoleon Bonaparte.

- Explore the Maison Bonaparte and the Imperial Chapel.

- Enjoy a leisurely walk along the waterfront promenade.

- Cost: Accommodation in Ajaccio can range from $80 to $200 per night.

Day 7: Departure

- Depending on your flight time, you may have some free time in the morning to explore Ajaccio further or do some last-minute shopping.

- Cost: The cost of departure will depend on your chosen method of transportation.

Please note that the costs provided are approximate and can vary depending on the season, availability, and level of comfort you prefer. Additionally, the itinerary can be adjusted based on your personal preferences and interests.

To get a more accurate cost estimate, it is recommended to research and compare accommodation prices, transportation costs, and any additional activities or meals you plan to include during your stay in Corsica.

A detailed 3 three days itinerary

Day 1: Arrival in Ajaccio

- Arrive in Ajaccio, the capital of Corsica, and explore the city's historical and cultural landmarks.

- Visit the Maison Bonaparte, the birthplace of Napoleon Bonaparte, and explore the old town.

- Enjoy a leisurely stroll along the palm-lined waterfront promenade.

- Cost: Accommodation in Ajaccio can range from $80 to $200 per night.

Day 2: Scenic Drive and Nature Exploration

- Rent a car and embark on a scenic drive along the coast to Porto-Vecchio.

- Stop at beautiful viewpoints and enjoy the stunning coastal landscapes.

- Arrive in Porto-Vecchio and spend the day exploring the town's historic center and charming streets.

- Relax on the nearby beaches of Palombaggia or Santa Giulia.

- Cost: Accommodation in Porto-Vecchio can range from $100 to $300 per night.

Day 3: Bonifacio and Natural Wonders

- Travel to Bonifacio, a picturesque town perched atop white limestone cliffs.

- Explore the historic citadel and wander through the narrow streets.

- Take a boat tour to discover the stunning limestone cliffs and hidden caves along the coastline.

- Visit the King of Aragon's Stairway and enjoy panoramic views of the sea.

- Cost: Accommodation in Bonifacio can range from $100 to $300 per night.

Please note that the costs provided are approximate and can vary depending on the season, availability, and level of comfort you prefer. Additionally, the itinerary can be adjusted based on your personal preferences and interests.

To get a more accurate cost estimate, it is recommended to research and compare accommodation prices, transportation costs, and any additional activities or meals you plan to include during your stay in Corsica.

Reliable book source for your Corsica travel

1. Booking.com: Booking.com is a popular online platform that offers a wide range of accommodation options, including hotels, apartments, villas, and guesthouses. It provides detailed descriptions, user reviews, and competitive prices.

2. Airbnb: Airbnb is a trusted platform for booking unique accommodations, such as apartments, houses, and private rooms. It allows you to connect directly with hosts and provides a more personalized and local experience.

3. Expedia: Expedia is a well-known online travel agency that offers comprehensive travel services, including flights, hotels, vacation packages, and car rentals. It provides a user-friendly interface and allows you to compare prices from various providers.

4. Hotels.com: Hotels.com specializes in hotel bookings and offers a wide selection of properties, from budget to luxury options. It provides detailed hotel information, customer reviews, and competitive rates.

5. Tripadvisor: Tripadvisor is a reliable source for researching and booking accommodations, as well as finding reviews and recommendations from fellow travelers. It aggregates information from multiple sources and provides a comprehensive overview of available options.

It's always a good idea to compare prices and read reviews from multiple sources before making a booking decision. Additionally, visiting the official websites of specific hotels or accommodations can sometimes offer exclusive deals or promotions.

Emergency contact numbers

Medical Emergencies:

- Emergency Medical Services: 15

- SAMU (Medical Emergency): 15

- SOS Doctors (House Call Service): 3624

Police and Security:

- Police Emergency: 17

- Gendarmerie (Local Police): 17

- Coast Guard: 196

- Fire Brigade: 18

Roadside Assistance:

- Automobile Club: 0800 052 052

- National Breakdown Service: 116 117

Other Emergency Contacts:

- European Emergency Number: 112 (can be used for all emergencies)

- Mountain Rescue: 112

- Sea Rescue: 196

- Poison Control Center: 0800 59 59 59

It's important to note that emergency contact numbers may vary or be subject to change. It is advisable to check with local authorities or your accommodation provider for the most up-to-date contact information.

30 dos and don'ts for your Corsica travel

Dos in Corsica

1. Do greet people with a polite "Bonjour" (hello) or "Bonsoir" (good evening) when entering a shop, restaurant, or other public places.

2. Do try to speak a few basic French phrases or greetings, as it shows respect for the local culture.

3. Do dress modestly when visiting churches or religious sites. Cover your shoulders and avoid wearing beach attire in such places.

4. Do sample the local cuisine, including Corsican charcuterie, cheeses, and wines. Embrace the gastronomic delights of the island.

5. Do respect the environment and nature. Take care not to litter, and consider participating in eco-friendly activities or tours.

6. Do learn about Corsican history and culture. Visit museums, historical sites, and attend cultural events to gain a deeper understanding of the island.

7. Do explore the hidden gems of Corsica, such as remote beaches, charming villages, and natural wonders, to truly appreciate its beauty.

8. Do engage in outdoor activities like hiking, swimming, and boating to experience the diverse landscapes and coastal beauty of Corsica.

9. Do try to learn a few phrases in the Corsican language to interact with locals and show interest in their culture.

10. Do respect private property and obtain permission before entering someone's land for hiking or other activities.

Don'ts in Corsica

1. Don't greet people with a simple "Hi" or "Hello" without using the appropriate French greetings. It's considered impolite.

2. Don't ignore the local customs and laws. Familiarize yourself with the do's and don'ts to avoid any misunderstandings or offense.

3. Don't engage in loud or disruptive behavior, especially in residential areas or during quiet hours. Respect the peacefulness of the island.

4. Don't make excessive noise or play loud music on the beaches, as it may disturb other beachgoers.

5. Don't feed or disturb wildlife, including stray animals. Appreciate them from a distance and refrain from interfering with their natural habitats.

6. Don't engage in disrespectful or offensive behavior towards Corsican traditions, customs, or symbols.

7. Don't expect shops and businesses to be open during siesta hours (usually from 12:00 PM to 3:00 PM). Plan your activities accordingly.

8. Don't touch or climb on ancient monuments, historical artifacts, or protected natural formations. Preserve the island's heritage for future generations.

9. Don't smoke in prohibited areas, including indoor public spaces, beaches, and certain outdoor locations. Observe designated smoking areas and respect non-smoking rules.

10. Don't ignore warnings and signs indicating restricted areas, dangerous terrain, or prohibited activities. Follow instructions for your safety.

11. Don't leave valuables unattended or visible in your car. Take necessary precautions to prevent theft.

12. Don't haggle excessively in shops or markets. Bargaining is not a common practice in Corsica, except in specific situations.

13. Don't discuss sensitive political or historical topics unless you have a good understanding of the local context and are engaging in respectful conversation.

14. Don't assume that everyone speaks English. While some people do, it's always appreciated to make an effort to communicate in French or use simple phrases.

15. Don't take photographs of people without their consent, especially in private or intimate settings.

16. Don't expect fast-paced service in restaurants. Corsican dining is typically relaxed and focused on enjoying the meal and the company.

17. Don't remove or damage natural resources, such as plants, rocks, or shells. Leave them as you found them for others to enjoy.

18. Don't drive under the influence of alcohol or drugs. Follow traffic rules and drive responsibly.

19. Don't rush or be impatient when interacting with locals. Embrace the slower pace of life in Corsica and enjoy the laid-back atmosphere.

20. Don't leave your trash behind. Dispose of it properly in designated bins or take it with you to maintain the cleanliness of the island.

10 important money saving tips

1. Plan your trip during the shoulder seasons: Consider visiting Corsica during the spring or autumn months when the weather is still pleasant but the tourist crowds are thinner. This can result in lower accommodation and flight prices.

2. Book accommodation in advance: Take advantage of early booking discounts and secure affordable accommodation options before they fill up. Look for budget-friendly hotels, guesthouses, or self-catering apartments.

3. Use public transportation: Corsica has a reliable and affordable public transportation system, including buses and trains. Opt for public transportation instead of renting a car to save on fuel, parking, and rental costs.

4. Cook your own meals: Take advantage of local markets and grocery stores to buy fresh produce and ingredients. Prepare some of your meals in your accommodation to save on dining expenses.

5. Explore free attractions and activities: Corsica offers stunning natural landscapes and beautiful beaches that can be enjoyed without spending a fortune. Take advantage of hiking trails, public beaches, and free sightseeing spots.

6. Pack a picnic: Instead of eating out for every meal, pack a picnic with local produce and enjoy a meal in a scenic outdoor setting. This not only saves money but also allows you to savor the beauty of Corsica.

7. Research and compare prices: Before making any bookings or purchases, research different options and compare prices. Look for deals, discounts, or package offers that can help you save money on accommodations, activities, or transportation.

8. Carry a refillable water bottle: Corsica has numerous natural springs where you can refill your water bottle for free. This saves money on buying bottled water and reduces plastic waste.

9. Take advantage of free walking tours or guided hikes: Many cities and towns in Corsica offer free walking tours or guided hikes that provide insight into the local history, culture, and natural surroundings. Joining these activities can be both informative and cost-effective.

10. Avoid unnecessary souvenirs: While it's tempting to buy souvenirs, be mindful of your budget. Focus on collecting meaningful and unique items that truly capture the essence of Corsica. Avoid overspending on generic trinkets.

Best time to travel to Corsica for the best prices

The best time to travel to Corsica for the best prices would generally be during the shoulder seasons, which are the periods just before and after the peak tourist season. Here are some recommendations:

1. Spring (April to June): This is a great time to visit Corsica as the weather is pleasant, and the island is covered in beautiful blooms. Prices for accommodations and flights are generally lower than in the peak summer season.

2. Autumn (September to October): Another ideal time to visit Corsica is during the autumn months when the summer crowds have dispersed. The weather remains warm, and you can enjoy the island's natural beauty without the peak season prices.

It's important to note that prices can vary depending on specific events, holidays, and availability, so it's recommended to compare prices across different booking platforms and be flexible with your travel dates. Additionally, booking in advance or taking advantage of last-minute deals can also help you find better prices.

Keep in mind that while traveling during the shoulder seasons may offer better prices, some tourist services and attractions may have reduced operating hours or limited availability compared to the peak season. However, if you're looking to save money and avoid the crowds, the shoulder seasons can be a great option for your Corsica trip.

20 Important Safety Tips

1. Familiarize yourself with the local laws and customs of Corsica before your trip to ensure you respect cultural norms and avoid any legal issues.

2. Keep your personal belongings secure at all times. Use a money belt or hidden pouch to carry your valuables, and be cautious of pickpockets in crowded areas.

3. Make copies of important documents such as your passport, ID, and travel insurance. Keep one set with you and leave another set with a trusted person back home.

4. Stay updated on the current weather conditions and any potential natural hazards. Check weather forecasts and heed any warnings or advisories issued by local authorities.

5. Stay hydrated, especially during the summer months when temperatures can be high. Carry a reusable water bottle and drink plenty of fluids throughout the day.

6. Protect yourself from the sun by wearing sunscreen, a hat, and sunglasses. Seek shade during the hottest hours of the day and reapply sunscreen regularly.

7. Be cautious when swimming in the sea, as some beaches may have strong currents or underwater hazards. Observe warning signs and swim in designated areas with lifeguards present.

8. Follow safety instructions and guidelines for outdoor activities such as hiking, rock climbing, and water sports. Use proper equipment, stay on marked trails, and be aware of your physical limitations.

9. Keep emergency contact numbers handy, including local police, ambulance services, and your embassy or consulate.

10. When driving, familiarize yourself with local traffic rules and regulations. Observe speed limits, wear seatbelts, and avoid driving under the influence of alcohol or drugs.

11. Be cautious when hiking in remote areas, as terrain conditions can be challenging. Inform someone of your hiking plans and consider hiring a local guide for more difficult trails.

12. Respect wildlife and their habitats. Do not approach or feed wild animals, and be mindful of protected areas or nature reserves where additional restrictions may apply.

13. Stay informed about any political or social unrest that may be occurring in the region and avoid areas where demonstrations or protests are taking place.

14. Be aware of your surroundings, especially in crowded tourist areas. Stay vigilant against potential scams or thefts and report any suspicious activity to the authorities.

15. Carry a basic first aid kit with essential supplies, including band-aids, antiseptic wipes, pain relievers, and any necessary prescription medications.

16. Follow health and hygiene practices, including frequent handwashing, especially before meals. Be cautious with food and water consumption, opting for bottled water and eating at reputable establishments.

17. Dress appropriately when visiting religious sites or conservative areas. Respect local customs by covering your shoulders and knees.

18. Be cautious when consuming alcohol, especially in unfamiliar surroundings. Drink responsibly and be mindful of your personal safety and well-being.

19. Stay connected with your loved ones by sharing your travel plans and checking in regularly. Inform them of your whereabouts and provide emergency contact information.

20. Trust your instincts and use common sense throughout your trip. If a situation feels unsafe or uncomfortable, remove yourself from it and seek assistance if needed.

Remember, while these safety tips are important, don't let them overshadow the enjoyment of your trip. Stay informed, be prepared, and embrace the beauty and experiences that Corsica has to offer.

165

CHAPTER SIX

Conclusion

In conclusion, Corsica is a captivating destination that offers a wealth of natural beauty, cultural experiences, and thrilling outdoor activities. With its rugged mountains, pristine beaches, charming villages, and rich history, Corsica has something to offer every traveler.

From exploring the majestic Calanques de Piana and the UNESCO-listed Scandola Nature Reserve to indulging in the delectable Corsican cuisine and immersing in the island's unique traditions, visitors are sure to be enchanted by the diverse range of experiences that await them.

Whether you're seeking adventure through hiking, rock climbing, or water sports, or you prefer to relax on idyllic beaches and savor local delicacies, Corsica caters to all interests and preferences. The island's warm Mediterranean climate, coupled with its welcoming locals and stunning landscapes, make it an ideal destination for a memorable vacation.

With this comprehensive travel guide, you'll have all the information you need to plan an unforgettable trip to Corsica. From transportation and accommodation options to detailed insights into the top attractions, activities, and dining experiences, this guide will serve as your trusted companion throughout your journey.

So, pack your bags, embark on an adventure, and immerse yourself in the beauty and charm of Corsica. Whether you're a nature enthusiast, a history buff, or a seeker of unique cultural experiences, Corsica promises to leave you with lasting memories and a desire to return to this enchanting island time and time again.

Bon voyage!

Printed in Great Britain
by Amazon